# THE CRITICISM OF EXPERIENCE

# THE
# CRITICISM OF EXPERIENCE

by

## D. J. B. HAWKINS

LONDON
**SHEED & WARD**
1945

NIHIL OBSTAT: R. PHILLIPS
CENSOR DEPUTATUS

IMPRIMATUR: S. BANFI, V.G.

SOUTHWARCI, DIE 20A JUNII 1945

FIRST PUBLISHED 1945
BY SHEED AND WARD, LTD.
110/111 FLEET STREET
LONDON, E.C.4

THIS BOOK IS PRODUCED
IN COMPLETE CONFORMITY
WITH THE WAR ECONOMY AGREEMENT

PRINTED IN GREAT BRITAIN
BY PURNELL AND SONS, LTD.
PAULTON (SOMERSET) AND LONDON

# FOREWORD

Two main groups of questions belong to a complete theory of knowledge. The one forms the strictly philosophical content of logic. It might be said simply to be logic, but that logic as it is actually taught and written consists partly in discussions of genuine philosophical import and partly in a kind of linguistic gymnastic. The latter is not to be despised; its possibility depends on philosophical principles, and it might, with the minimum of necessary philosophical explanation, be taught with advantage in the higher classes of schools. Its benefits in its own sphere are similar to those of physical training. Persons who have not been apprenticed to it suffer quite noticeably in argument from a lack of suppleness both in thought and in the use of language.

The strictly philosophical part of logic is obviously, however, more important. The nature of thinking and of the judgment, the validity of universal concepts, the scope of implication and of reasoning—these are all questions of great philosophical moment, and lead straight to the problems of metaphysics. To these and other logical questions philosophers have always devoted a good deal of attention, and the ancient and mediaeval thinkers have as much to say about them as the moderns.

The questions belonging to the second group are more concrete. They concern what sorts of things we are able to know, and how we come to know them. They examine the credentials of the kind of knowledge which common sense takes for granted, and may, therefore, be said to constitute a criticism of experience. A systematic criticism of experience is the novel characteristic of philosophy since Descartes. While previous thinkers had treated these questions incidentally and incompletely, Descartes made it clear that there was a new territory for philosophy to conquer by treating them systematically and with full rigour.

It would consequently be anachronistic to look for a full answer to these problems in thinkers before Descartes. Nevertheless the ancient and mediaeval philosophers cannot be neglected when we are dealing with this field, for no serious philosophy is wholly without bearing upon it. Moreover, it is instructive to examine what earlier thinkers took for granted. For the rational instinct of man is sometimes sounder than his explicit theorizing, and, although what was at one time taken for granted may turn out to be erroneous, it yet may in other cases suggest the proper outcome of a later analysis.

Still, our principal concern in the criticism of experience must be with philosophy since Descartes. Although the greater part of the Cartesian system has perished, the new direction which its author gave to philosophical inquiry remains. The view that the first task of philosophy is to provide a criticism of experience is dominant especially in the classical line of philosophers writing in English, in Locke, Berkeley and Hume, in Reid and Hamilton, and, in our own day, in G. E. Moore and thinkers of similar inspiration. Just at the present moment too many English philosophers seem to have lost heart, and are occupying themselves with purely linguistic analysis, but it is to be hoped that this is only a passing phase and that real philosophy will revive.

The vital period of development in the criticism of experience comprises roughly the seventeenth and eighteenth centuries, from Descartes to Kant on the Continent and to Reid and Hamilton in these islands. In this department philosophy has since been living mainly on the problems enucleated, and even on the solutions put forward, during this period. While there have, of course, been endless refinements of detail, the outline map of the region still bears much the appearance which it then assumed. That is why a treatment of the subject which aims at avoiding prolixity must lay its principal emphasis on the thinkers of this period.

In the course of our inquiry we shall have constantly to be pointing out the inadequacies of the classical philosophers of modern times. Yet we should not be deficient in respect and admiration for the candour and tenacity with which they explored the contents of the mind. Their positive results bring into relief those fundamental evidences which cannot be overlooked; their inadequacies show in what direction their successors must pursue their researches in order to supply what is still required.

There are those who in philosophy look for something more inspiring than a criticism of experience, and grow restive with the unending complications which philosophers introduce when they ask what we mean by saying that this is a table. It is, indeed, a mistake to suppose that the criticism of experience is the end of philosophy, but it is undoubtedly an essential part of the beginning. Every building needs a foundation, and, the higher the building would rise, the deeper its foundations must be.

# CONTENTS

# THE CRITICISM OF EXPERIENCE

## CHAPTER I

## KNOWLEDGE AND REALITY

### § 1

KNOWING in its widest generality is too simple a notion for definition. Specific kinds and ways of knowing can be defined, but the elementary concept of knowing which all these presuppose must be discovered by reflection on experience. If you had to explain to someone what red is, you would show him an instance of it, and tell him to look at it. Similarly, with knowing in general, the philosopher can only tell his hearers or readers to look at it introspectively, and to see whether their analytic reflection confirms what he has to say about it or not.

What your reflection is now called upon to substantiate is the fundamental relation of knowing to fact. To know is primarily to know something, and something means a reality. A great many objects which are not real in the ordinary sense of the word enter into our mental view, but they could not do so unless we were first aware of things which are real in the ordinary sense. They could not do so, indeed, unless they bore themselves some analogy to things which are real in the ordinary sense.

Justice is not a reality in the usual sense of the word. There are just persons and just acts, but, with all respect to Plato, there does not exist justice which is simply justice by itself. But, when you talk about justice, it

11

is very plain that what you are really talking about is possibly just persons and just acts. The applications are only obliquely present to your mind, but you would be talking about nothing at all unless the applications were possible. So it is with all abstractions that, when you talk about them, the only final meaning which can be given to what you say is in terms of their real applications.

The character of Hamlet is an inhabitant of your mental world. There may have been a real Hamlet, but the Hamlet with whom you are familiar is a figure imagined by Shakespeare. Nevertheless, this figure is not entirely and irremediably detached from reality. There must have been a real Shakespeare to imagine him. Even if this Shakespeare had been, as people have strangely supposed, identical with Bacon, there must have been a real Bacon. The writer of *Hamlet* must have made real marks on paper, which are approximately reproduced in modern editions of Shakespeare in order to convey his imagination to you. And his very imaginative conception of the character of Hamlet must have been based in the end on human nature as he observed it in the real persons whom he met. Fictions are inexplicable without a foundation in reality.

Primarily, then, to know is to be aware of something real, and objects of mind which are not real in the usual sense of the word are secondary and have to be explained in terms of primary objects which are unambiguously real. Knowing is, of its very nature, related to fact and rooted in fact. Moreover, it is, of its nature, a way of escape from subjectivity, from the fatality by which you are merely what you yourself are. You cannot *be* more than you are, but you can *know* things other than yourself. The thinking mind, as Aristotle profoundly remarks, is in a certain way all things.[1] This is to say that, although a thinking being is literally only what it is, there is in the nature of know-

[1] Aristotle: *De Anima*, III, viii, 431b.

ing no limit to the range of reality which may be mentally embraced and assimilated. If this general view of knowledge is adequately appreciated, the thinker will be spared the peril of a false start in the criticism of experience, a false start which many philosophers have nevertheless incurred.

## § 2

The most harmful type of mistake which this fundamental realism enables you to avoid is that of supposing in the primitive act of awareness some intermediary between knowledge and reality, some specifically mental object which has first to be known and only beyond which reality comes to be known, unless, maybe, reality has to be regarded as unknowable. This mistake has given rise to the different varieties of phenomenalism or epistemological idealism. It cannot be called idealism without a qualification, for there is also that metaphysical idealism which is the doctrine that all reality has a mental character and is perfectly compatible with a realistic theory of knowledge. Phenomenalism, or idealism in the epistemological sense, appears in a comparatively simple form with Descartes and Locke, and in a much more complex form with Kant. Like all mistakes which have had a profound influence on the history of thought, it can be presented with a certain plausibility.

It would not be unfamiliar in ordinary speech to say that knowledge consists of the ideas which we have about things. Our ideas have not always turned out to be correct. The discovery that an opinion which we have hitherto entertained is wrong, is not so rare an experience that we can dispense ourselves from a rational suspicion that some of our present opinions are wrong too. It seems, then, that there is a gulf to be bridged between ideas and opinions on the one hand and things and facts on the other. When these correspond, the ideas and opinions are true; when they fail to correspond, the ideas and opinions are false. In order to verify ideas and opinions, we have to compare them with things and facts. But how are we to get outside our own ideas? When we turn our attention to a thing, we are at once forming an idea of it. There seems to be always a mental object between ourselves and reality. If we believe that this situation persists upon ultimate analysis, and that our task is to find a bridge between ideas and things, we are phenomenalists.

Historically, this manner of putting the problem of knowledge makes its appearance with Descartes, but it bears to two mediaeval doctrines a relation which explains how Descartes came to construct this hurdle for himself to get over. The mediaeval Aristotelians had described the process of perception in terms which were based on Aristotle's dictum that sensation is the reception of sensible forms (εἴδων) without matter.[1] Using *species* for εἶδος, they said that in perceptual experience the percipient was actuated by the *species* of the object. While, in the most authentic mediaeval thought, no misunderstanding was possible, for this assimilation of subject to object preceded the act of perception, which was just simply an act of awareness of the object, many of the later scholastics thought of this assimilation as residing in the perceptual act itself, so that to perceive was necessarily to produce a *species* or image of the object. They had no doubt, of course, that the *species* was not the object of perception. It was a determination of the subject by means of which there was a direct perception of the external object, and came itself to be known only by analytic reflection on the perceptual process. Nevertheless it is easy to see that, if you begin to think of perception as the production of an image of the object, there is a very real temptation to believe that you must be aware

[1] Aristotle: *De Anima*, II, xii, 424a.

of the image first and of the object only indirectly through the image.

William of Ockham, in the fourteenth century, while rejecting the terminology of *species*, speaks of percepts and concepts as signs. Once again, it seems clear that Ockham did not think that the sign was the immediate object of knowledge, and that the thing was known after the sign. The thing, in his view, was directly known through the sign. Yet what we normally call a sign is something through the knowledge of which the thing signified comes to be known, and it was fatally easy to interpret Ockham's terminology in this way. We notice the tendency at once in his more radical disciples, such as Nicholas of Autrecourt. By a degeneration, then, of these two mediaeval doctrines Descartes was led to envisage the problem of knowledge in terms of images which were mental signs of their objects, and whose connection with their objects had to be justified.

Descartes does not apply this view to the whole of knowledge, for, as everyone knows, it is a fundamental point in his system that we have, by reflection on the act of thought, a direct knowledge of the self as mind. *Cogito, ergo sum.* But, as far as external things and even the body of the percipient are concerned, we begin with representative ideas, and must find grounds for asserting that the things exist which they represent. Descartes finds a way out in our irresistible tendency to believe in the existence of the material world, combined with the veracity of God, who could not have created us with this tendency if the material world were not real. Not all our ideas, however, are thus guaranteed by the divine veracity. It is only extension and movement which we cannot help attributing to material things. The inclination to attribute colours, sounds and the other sense-qualities to the external world is not irresistible, and can be corrected by reflection. Hence, in the end, the ideas of colour, sound and the rest cease to be images or representations; they are simply modifications of the mind. The pure doctrine of representative ideas subsists only in respect of extension and movement.

Locke, although an opponent of Descartes on some questions, proceeds from a similar viewpoint in his theory of perception. We have ideas both of the primary qualities of extension and its modes, and of the secondary qualities of colour, sound and the rest. Locke then sets out to establish that the ideas of the primary qualities are resemblances of external objects, while the ideas of the secondary qualities are not. If this is so, the ideas of the secondary qualities are not to be regarded as images, and the doctrine of representative ideas receives the same final restriction as it received from Descartes.

Our present business, however, is not with the details of Descartes's or Locke's system but with the doctrine of representative ideas in the abstract. Is it a necessary or appropriate way of approaching the problem of knowledge? It seems evident that it is not. If it were sound, it would face us with the problem of comparing what purports to be an image with a prototype of which, by hypothesis, we have no knowledge except through an image, whether this image or another. That this is an embarrassing position is obvious. But then we ask ourselves how we are supposed to know that our ideas purport to be images of external things. When we recognize something to be an image of something else, it implies that we are already acquainted with what it represents or with something like it. A picture would be merely an abstract design of form and colour unless we had some acquaintance with the things which it represents, or at any rate with the elements which make these up. We have not a direct acquaintance with centaurs, but we can recognize pictures of them because we have a direct acquaintance with horses and with human beings. We could not, however, even suspect that anything was an image of, or resembled, something else unless we had some previous knowledge of the class of thing which we took it to resemble.

How does this stand with the doctrine of representative ideas? This doctrine asks us to believe that, before we have any acquaintance with material things, we can recognize that our ideas purport to be images of them. This is evidently impossible, and, even on the hypothesis that our ideas were, in fact, images of material things, we could never, if we were confined to such ideas as our initial data, know that they were images. We should regard them simply as qualities of the mind and remain entirely ignorant of the existence of the material world. Hence the theory that, whether over the whole realm of knowledge or in relation to some specific class of objects, we begin with a set of ideas or representations whose correspondence with reality has to be established, cannot be upheld. Awareness is primitively of real facts, whatever may be the sphere of reality to which these facts belong.

### § 3

Kant's phenomenalism, being of a more subtle and thoroughgoing kind than that of Descartes, must be discussed separately. Kant was painfully aware of what had happened to philosophy during the century between Descartes and himself. A series of thinkers had struggled to find a bridge between the self and the external world, and had only involved themselves in increasing difficulties. Their lack of success might well arouse the suspicion that they had been guilty of a false presupposition; at any rate that was Kant's diagnosis.

The assumption which Kant eventually decided that he ought to traverse was that the function of human mind was to know things as they are in themselves independently of our knowledge of them. With this preconception philosophers had racked their brains to find some way of escaping from their own subjectivity and assuring themselves of a real external world, and their efforts had failed. If you asked the philosopher, it would seem that genuine knowledge was impossible, yet mathematicians and scientists were increasing the sum of knowledge all the time.

When the philosophers were convicted of the falsity of their assumption, the contradiction would disappear. Philosophy would undergo its Copernican revolution and be put on the right track again. After all it was clear enough that you could not know anything without your knowledge being a factor in the situation. The activity of the mind itself must not be forgotten; the function of the speculative philosopher should, indeed, be to investigate how the mind collaborates in the construction of the object of knowledge.

Kant's supposed discovery was, then, that there is no speculative knowledge of things as they are in themselves, and that it is a mistake to believe that there ought to be such knowledge. We can know things only as they appear to our minds; the object of knowledge is an appearance or phenomenon, and a science is an organized system of phenomena. Not that the way in which anything appears to anybody is equally valid; the activity of thought has its proper laws to which it must submit. The common-sense distinction between appearance and reality has a meaning, but it becomes on analysis a distinction between two kinds of appearance. Mere appearance is one whose character is due to the personal and particular dispositions of the observer, while what we call reality is an appearance which presents itself in full accordance with the universal laws of thought. In this way both common-sense appearance and common-sense reality fall in the end within the field of appearances to us as distinguished from things as they are in themselves; it is vain to look for a knowledge of things as they are apart from our knowledge of them.

While the thing in itself necessarily remains outside the sphere of theoretical knowledge, Kant indignantly rejects the charge of subjectivism by maintaining that phenomena presenting themselves in accordance with the laws of mind are strictly objective. They are, in fact, the proper objects of human knowledge, and the system which recognizes this is the only possible antidote to scepticism and the only genuine foundation for the objective validity of the sciences. Moreover, Kant holds firmly that there are things in themselves, although the theoretical reason can say nothing about them as they are in themselves. Only the moral activity of the practical reason attains contact with reality as it is in itself. Phenomena cannot be asserted to resemble things in themselves, but they stand in some sense for them. Although the category of cause and effect is applicable only within the field of phenomena, the phenomena cannot but be regarded as the product of the joint activity, in some different sense of activity, of mind in itself and things in themselves. Thus Kant claims to hold the balance between naïve dogmatism and sceptical idealism.

In fact, of course, this is subjectivism with a vengeance; it is a complete reversal of the natural relationship between mind and reality. The verbal gymnastic which raises appearances to the dignity of objects is poor consolation for denying that we can know what anything is in itself or even what we are in ourselves. The *Critique of Pure Reason* contains discussions of specific questions which demand to be taken into account when those questions are raised; it remains in fact a pretty complete catalogue of the philosophical difficulties which arose in the seventeenth and eighteenth centuries, and which have continued to occupy a considerable share of the attention of philosophers since. Nevertheless its general view of the nature of knowledge can be rather summarily rejected for a reason parallel to that advanced in refutation of the doctrine of representative ideas.

For how, on Kant's principles, can we come to suspect that phenomena are phenomena? How do we know that they stand in some obscure way for things in themselves which we can never know? Before we know that something is a sign of something else, or stands for something else, we must have some acquaintance with the class of thing for which it stands. But, according to Kant, we have no speculative acquaintance with things in themselves, and the practical reason will not provide us with a standard of comparison, for it transcends phenomena already recognized as such. If Kant were right in holding that we cannot know things in themselves, what he calls phenomena would present themselves as mental modifications with their own reality, and we could have no notion that they stood in any sense for anything else. If we can contrast the appearance with the thing in itself, it can only be because we have some acquaintance with the thing in itself. Construction is a secondary activity of thought; its primary activity is an awareness of the real in its reality. This natural fundamental principle asserts itself against any attempt at denial. Kant's view of knowledge stands condemned because it reverses the necessary order of the notions of appearance and reality. Phenomenalism, whether in the simpler form of the doctrine of representative ideas or in the more subtle and complex shape in which it was put forward by Kant, contradicts the nature of experience as it reveals itself to reflection.

For appearance, on the occasions when the term can be appropriately used, always presupposes reality. If I say that this appears to be gold, there is a real somewhat of which I am already aware and which is the subject of my judgment. Even a mirage is a real visual datum, although it may appear to be more. When I say that this appears to be gold, I mean that this manifests some of the qualities of gold, so that I can pass a probable judgment that it really is gold. Since probable judgments are always compatible with error, I may discover that the appearance is illusory, and that the thing is only a clever imitation. In that case I contrast appearance with reality, but there would not even be appearance unless there were some factual evidence that the thing was what it appeared to be. Consequently, in the criticism of experience, we must look for the facts of which we are primitively aware, and, if we can discover genuinely primitive data, they will be indubitably real.

## § 4

Although phenomenalism is the extreme form of the subjectivist tendency, it does not exhaust the possible ravages of subjectivism. Hume cannot properly be called a phenomenalist, for his impressions and ideas, for what they are worth, seem to be real. But he will allow us to know nothing except impressions and ideas, which is to say sensations and images. Knowledge is thus reduced to bare consciousness and can almost be left out of account. It is not surprising that the nearest to Hume among contemporary philosophers, Bertrand Russell, should have come to throw doubt on the existence of consciousness itself.

The cause of the arbitrary dogma which restricts our awareness to sensations and images appears to be a psychological defect which renders a man incapable of attending in reflection to anything save the importunate multitude of sense-impressions. Since these belong to the subject which is conscious of them, it is thought that all awareness must be of the same kind. To make such an assertion, however, shows that the thinker has never really reflected on the nature of knowing at all, and disqualifies him from claiming to have reached a satisfactory philosophy.

Without going as far as Hume's denial that there can be genuine knowledge of anything except events in the history of the self, thinkers past counting have tacitly assumed that there cannot be any direct or immediate knowledge except of the self. They have assumed that it must be an inference which makes us acquainted with the external world. Apart from their doctrine of representative ideas, both Descartes and Locke are obviously looking for reasons in the data of consciousness which will enable them to conclude to the existence of things other than the self. Among the great names of modern times, only the Scottish philosophers of the school of Reid and Hamilton[1] have wholeheartedly accepted the possibility of a direct acquaintance with external reality.

Reason must, of course, be given before we can assert that we have, in fact, a direct knowledge of the external world, but it is important to see at once that there is no general ground in the nature of knowing why we should not have it. Knowing is, as we have said, a way of escape from subjectivity, from being merely oneself. There is no reason why it should not bring us into mental contact with other things at once and directly. There must, no doubt, be a modification of the self which makes such an intuition possible, but there is no reason why this should be related to the awareness of external things as premiss to conclusion.

A considerable measure of responsibility for the gratuitous assumptions against which we are protesting must be attributed to a rather crude spatialization of the notion of knowledge. Thought is an activity of the subject; it is in the mind. How, then, can it attain to facts outside the mind or the subject? But thought is not spatial; the mind has not in a literal sense an inside or an outside. There is no harm in speaking of thoughts as being in the mind, provided that we remember that we are not employing the term *in* spatially, but, in the sense in which we are employing it, there is no absurdity in supposing that something a million miles away from our bodies is in our minds. Hence there is no foundation

[1] Sir William Hamilton is especially worthy of attention on the subject. Cf. *Lectures on Metaphysics*, lect. xxv.

for any alleged principle that thought can only attain, or only directly attain, to facts about the self.

Adequate reflection, then, recognizes knowing as naturally focused upon reality, and as a means of transcending the separateness of the self. If the facts of experience turn out to demand it, it is entirely admissible to hold that we have genuine knowledge, and even direct knowledge, of the external world. With this conception of the relation of knowledge and reality there is more hope of finding an issue to the criticism of experience.

## CHAPTER II

# SENSATION

## § 1

If on a long view sensations appear among the humbler elements of experience, they nevertheless possess a vividness which attests their importance in the structure of human knowledge. In fact, they so overwhelmed Hume that he could not persuade himself that anything of a different sort existed. Without going to that length, we may well suggest that the type of philosopher who goes straight ahead to construct an elaborate metaphysical system without first accurately investigating the nature of sensation is running a considerable risk of building a castle in the air.

Sensations are intimately associated with the knowledge of the material world, but the basic characteristic of a material thing is to be a mass extended in three dimensions. The consideration of voluminous or spatial factors, together with that of time, will be deferred until we have dealt with sensation proper. This recognizes the distinction commonly made since Galileo and Descartes, and commonly described since Boyle and Locke as the distinction between the primary qualities of extension and its modes and the secondary qualities which are the specific contents of sensation. The distinction is really a legacy of Greek thought; it can be found in Democritus, and it corresponds with Aristotle's discrimination of the common from the proper sensibles.

In ordinary speech we count five senses, but it is evident that, if this is intended to be an exhaustive catalogue of the different types of sensation, the sense of touch must be held to comprise a rather heterogeneous collection of experiences. The sensations which we have upon contact with other bodies are here lumped in with the highly various kinds of sensation which, since we associate them with the condition of parts of the bodily organism, may more conveniently be distinguished as general or organic sensation. Sensations of heat and cold obviously possess a character of their own, and deserve to be discriminated as belonging to a special sense of temperature. We need not, however, concern ourselves with the varying ways in which psychologists divide the kinds of sensation; our point is simply that we are speaking of the whole range of sense-experience, whether in common-sense thinking we associate it more particularly with states of the organism or with the recognition of external objects.

Hearing, taste and smell call for no special remark at present, but sight is more complex, inasmuch as visual experience includes both light and colour on the one hand and a certain extension on the other. The precise relationship of visual extension to the extension of bodies can be treated only when we are dealing with the latter subject, but, while we are speaking of sensation, we cannot escape considering the whole visual datum, its extension as well as light and colour.

Our business is differentiated from that of the psychologist by having another purpose. While the psychologist is interested in sensations primarily as events in the history of a mind, the philosopher directs his chief attention to their function in the building of knowledge. Yet it may be remarked, in passing, that it is difficult to be a sound philosopher without being something of a psychologist, just as it is difficult to be a good psychologist without being something of a philosopher.

It is of greater importance to see that the work of the philosopher is logically prior to that of the physicist and the physiologist. For the physicist and the physiologist, investigating the material conditions of sensation, presuppose the existence of the material world and some general conception of its nature. The philosopher, on the other hand, inquiring how we come to know the material world at all, is not entitled to take anything about it for granted. It is only after he has completed his analysis that he can, in the philosophical sphere, say that it exists, and what it is like. He does not, of course, perversely attempt to doubt that the material world exists, but he refrains from assuming it for the purpose of his inquiry. It is evident that his common-sense beliefs suggest the direction of his thinking, but they must not prejudice his conclusions. While there is an antecedent probability that common-sense thinking approximately hits the mark, it is susceptible of correction as well as of greater precision.

§ 2

From the rejection of phenomenalism it follows that the contents of sensation are not merely appearances. They are real, and we can ask where their reality resides. More specifically, in the case of the qualities revealed by what are usually called the external senses, we can ask whether they are qualities of external material things. Is the awareness of them an instance of external perception or simply of consciousness, understood as the immediate awareness of the present self? When we look at the red carpet, there is present to us an expanse of red which is the content of visual sensation. This red expanse is certainly real and immediately present to us. Is its redness the redness of the carpet, or is the carpet red in another sense?

Many people might be tempted to invoke the aid of the physical sciences in answering this question. That sensation is preceded by a physical process in the medium between the external thing and the sentient subject, and that sensation does not occur until this whole process reaches the brain, might be regarded as a decisive argument that sensation does not reveal a quality of the external thing. But it has already been observed that physics and physiology are irrelevant to our inquiry, since they presuppose a notion of the material world whose foundations the philosopher is examining. Whatever results the philosopher may reach, no physical or physiological theory can govern the discussion through which the assumptions of these sciences are to be established or overturned. In any case physical processes can never provide an adequate explanation of the scope of a cognitive act which follows upon them. Hence the genuine philosophical questions can be answered only by an analytic scrutiny of experience.

The assertion that the qualities manifested in sensation are qualities of external objects is sometimes described as naïve realism. It would more properly be said that realism is naïve when this is taken for granted without examination or explicit assertion. As soon as the question is raised, it is seen at once that it would need highly sophisticated reasoning to support so paradoxical an assertion.

There was in fact, however, a stage in the history of thought when this was taken for granted, and the attempt made to explain vision on the assumption that the colours manifested in sensation were qualities of external objects. Such must have been the presupposition of the early Greek theory of the visual ray. The Pythagoreans first attributed vision to a ray which proceeded from the eye to the object and was reflected back from the object to the eye. Empedocles also speaks of fire issuing from the eye, but, since he explained vision, in common with the other senses, by means of emanations from the object perceived, it seems not improbable that he regarded vision as occurring when these emanations coalesced with the visual ray. This would bring his theory into agreement with that of Plato, who says that colour, being the result of the impact of the eye upon the motion proceeding from the external object, is something intermediate, belonging strictly neither to the subject nor to the object.[1] Of Plato's view Theophrastus remarks that it lies "midway between the theories of those who say that vision falls upon its object and of those who hold that something is borne from visible objects to the organ of sight".[2]

Thus, the visual ray theory soon underwent a process of complication, but it must, in its origin, have been based on the assumption of naïve realism. It is, indeed, in the case of vision that people are chiefly tempted to exteriorize the contents of their sensations. Hence we may consider vision first and ask ourselves whether it can at once and immediately be a perception of an external object.

The answer, however, is very obviously negative. The datum of vision possesses properties which we should not dream of attributing to a material thing. When we look at the table, what we strictly see becomes larger as we approach and smaller as we move away. It changes colour in different lights. When we examine railway lines receding into the distance, what we can properly be said to see is a pair, not of parallel, but of convergent lines. These would be exceedingly disconcerting properties to attribute to the table or to the railway lines themselves.

The conclusion cannot be evaded by saying that under different conditions we are aware of a different selection of the real properties of the distant object. For the datum of vision is not a mere appearance but something real, and this real thing really differs in size and colour under different conditions, although no one would assert that the distant object was changing in a corresponding way. When we look at the railway lines,

---

[1] Plato: *Theaetetus*, 153 E—154 A.

[2] Theophrastus: *De Sensibus* § 5, ed. and trans. by G. M. Stratton in *Theophrastus and the Greek Physiological Psychology before Aristotle*, p. 71. For the whole theory of the visual ray cf. J. I. Beare: *Greek Theories of Elementary Cognition from Alcmaeon to Aristotle*, pp. 12–18, 44–47.

vision presents us with real lines which really converge. Hence not only do the properties of the visual datum not exhaust the properties of the material thing to which we relate it, but they are incompatible with what we suppose a material thing to be.

Similarly, in the case of sound, the real sound of which we are immediately aware really becomes louder as we approach the resonant object and softer as we move away. But there is comparatively little temptation, if we reflect at all, to exteriorize sensations of sound; it is only with sight, which we have, long before the age of reflection, grown accustomed to employ as our main source of information about distant objects, that it may require more than a moment's thought to recognize that the visual datum itself is not a quality of an external thing. With the other senses scarcely any such temptation exists. We can hardly be inclined to assert that the orange itself possesses those qualities of taste and smell which are present to us when we eat an orange. Nor do we suppose that the fire possesses the sensible quality of heat, or the ice the sensible quality of cold. All these qualities, indeed, are pleasant or painful in some degree. It is not simply the awareness of them which is pleasant or painful; we can be aware that it is extremely cold at the North Pole without needing to put on an overcoat. What is pleasant or painful is the actual possession of such qualities. Therefore they can be possessed only by a sentient subject capable of feeling pleasure or pain.

Finally, when we reflect on sensation simply for what it is in itself, we find it to be an experience of elementary simplicity. It does not include or presuppose any awareness of a spatial world. The data of sensation are not spatial objects; they do not occupy a place; they are not distant from us or from one another. They are not only mentally present to the awareness of them, as external objects are, but they are present in their physical reality. This is to say that they can only belong to the subject of that awareness. Reflection informs us that we possess the qualities of sensation as well as being aware of them. This is the clue to the peculiar vividness which the awareness of sensation enjoys; the sensation and the awareness are a unity in the sense that they belong to the same subject.

It is in this way that we can speak of sensations as subjective. Nothing, as we have seen, can be subjective in the sense that it is a mere appearance, a mere function of the awareness of it. Sensations are subjective only inasmuch as they belong to the subject which is aware of them. Sensations, then, are real, but they are objects of consciousness, of the immediate awareness of the present self.

§ 3

This conclusion is very evident on reflection, and, when we glance at the history of thought on the matter, we find that there is a considerable measure of agreement among philosophers about it. Apart from those thinkers who have succumbed to a phenomenalistic approach and thereby incurred a really crippling subjectivism from which there is no escape but which cannot reasonably be upheld, philosophers have generally seen more or less clearly that sense-qualities can be attributed only to the sentient subject.

When Democritus says that the only genuine knowledge is of spatial characters and contemptuously relegates sense-qualities to the region of the spurious, he is expressing himself inaccurately, for sense-qualities are themselves also genuine objects of knowledge. Behind his faulty statement, however, we can divine a just recognition of the subjectivity of sensation. For his purpose is to describe the material world, and he means that sense-qualities cannot be intrinsically attributed to material things. In Plato we find a similar recognition and a similar exaggeration, for the burden of his dis-

SENSATION

cussion in the *Theaetetus* is that sensible things are not
genuine objects of knowledge and must be transcended
before real knowledge begins.

Aristotle, with his firm grasp of the real world in its
integrity, restores sense-qualities as objects of knowledge
but undoubtedly regards them as belonging to the
sentient subject. It is curious that his doctrine on the
matter has sometimes been misunderstood, notably by
so distinguished an authority as Beare, who holds that
he believed the proper sensibles to be qualities of external
objects.[1] No one has yet improved on Hamilton's
exposition of Aristotle's real view,[2] but Aristotle's own
statements are by themselves sufficiently clear and
precise.[3]

"The actuality of sense-object and of sensation is one
and the same, although what each is differs; I mean,
for example, the actuality of sound and the actuality
of hearing."[4] Hearing and sound have a different
meaning, since hearing designates the activity of the
subject, while sound refers to the pure objective datum
or may contain an implicit reference to the external
stimulus. Nevertheless, Aristotle says, it is one and
the same actual fact which is referred to in both
cases.

"If, then, the movement, or the acting and being
acted upon, has its reality in that which is affected by
the action, the actuality of both sound and hearing must
reside in that which was potentially hearing; for the
actuality of acting and moving occurs in that which
suffers the action."[5] Aristotle, recognizing sensation as
the result of an external stimulus, applies his familiar

[1] Beare: *op. cit.*, pp. 234–5.
[2] Sir W. Hamilton, in his edition of *Reid*, Note D., pp. 826–830.
[3] Aristotle: *De Anima*, III, ii, 425b–426a.
[4] ἡ δὲ τοῦ αἰσθητοῦ ἐνέργεια καὶ τῆς αἰσθήσεως ἡ αὐτὴ μέν ἐστι καὶ μία, τὸ δ'εἶναι οὐ ταὐτὸν αὐταῖς· λέγω δ'οἷον ψόφος ὁ κατ' ἐνέργειαν καὶ ἀκοὴ ἡ κατ' ἐνέργειαν.
[5] εἰ δ'ἔστιν ἡ κίνησις καὶ ἡ ποίησις καὶ τὸ πάθος ἐν τῷ ποιουμένῳ, ἀνάγκη καὶ τὸν ψόφον καὶ τὴν ἀκοὴν τὴν κατ' ἐνέργειαν ἐν τῇ κατὰ δύναμιν εἶναι· ἡ γὰρ τοῦ ποιητικοῦ καὶ κινητικοῦ ἐνέργεια ἐν τῷ πάσχοντι ἐγγίνεται.

31

general principle that the reality of an action resides in that which suffers the action; the agent is so designated by an external causal relation to the effect, which is a new reality in the patient. Hence the new reality which comes to be in sensation, whether, for example, it be called sound or hearing, resides in the sentient subject which suffers the stimulus.

"Since the actuality of both sense-object and sense is the same, although what each is differs, actual hearing and sound must pass away or continue to be together; and the same is true of flavour and tasting and the rest. But this is not necessarily true in terms of potentiality, although the earlier investigators of nature were mistaken about it, thinking that white and black were nothing at all apart from sight, and flavour nothing apart from tasting. In one way they were right, but in another wrong; for sensation and sense-object being taken in two ways, either potentially or actually, what they said is valid in the latter meaning but not in the former."[1] Since sound and hearing are one thing, they must come to be and pass away simultaneously. Nevertheless, Aristotle makes due allowance for common-sense language, which is implicitly used in terms of potentiality. We can continue to call an external object white or black, because it is permanently capable of provoking a sensation of white or black, just as we can say that we possess sight even when our eyes are shut, because we are capable of seeing if we open them. Thus the appearance of paradox in the denial by Democritus that sense-qualities have any reality apart from sensation can be avoided; they have potential reality in the thing which is able to stimulate them. As far, however, as

[1] ἐπεὶ δὲ μία μέν ἐστιν ἐνέργεια ἡ τοῦ αἰσθητοῦ καὶ ἡ τοῦ αἰσθητικοῦ, τὸ δ' εἶναι ἕτερον, ἀνάγκη ἅμα φθείρεσθαι καὶ σώζεσθαι τὴν οὕτω λεγομένην ἀκοὴν καὶ ψόφον, καὶ χυμὸν δὴ καὶ γεῦσιν καὶ τὰ ἄλλα ὁμοίως· τὰ δὲ κατὰ δύναμιν λεγόμενα οὐκ ἀνάγκη, ἀλλ' οἱ πρότερον φυσιολόγοι τοῦτο οὐ καλῶς ἔλεγον, οὐθὲν οἰόμενοι οὔτε λευκὸν οὔτε μέλαν εἶναι ἄνευ ὄψεως, οὐδὲ χυμὸν ἄνευ γεύσεως. τῇ μὲν γὰρ ἔλεγον ὀρθῶς, τῇ δ' οὐκ ὀρθῶς· διχῶς γὰρ λεγομένης τῆς αἰσθήσεως καὶ τοῦ αἰσθητοῦ, τῶν μέν κατὰ δύναμιν τῶν δὲ κατ' ἐνέργειαν, ἐπὶ τούτων μὲν συμβαίνει τὸ λεχθέν, ἐπὶ δὲ τῶν ἑτέρων οὐ συμβαίνει.

the main point is concerned, which is their actual reality, Aristotle is at one with Democritus.

Aristotle's whole discussion may also be related to the view expressed by Plato in the *Theaetetus*, that black and white come to be as a result of the collaboration of the eye with the appropriate motion from the external object. While Plato leaves sense-qualities almost literally in the air, belonging strictly neither to subject nor to object, Aristotle preserves the notion of sensation as a unity due to the collaboration of subject and object, but assigns the function of receptive power to the subject and that of active stimulation to the external object. Then, applying the principle that the reality of an action resides in the patient, he concludes that the actuality of both sensation and sense-quality belongs to the subject. The external object is only potentially black or white, not merely potentially perceptible black or white but potentially black or white in the sense that it is capable of stimulating these sensations. There can be no doubt, therefore, that Aristotle regarded the proper sensibles as qualities of the sentient subject.

It follows that two observers do not sense numerically the same quality, although the source of their sensations may be the same.[1] If there were no living beings, there would be neither sense-quality nor sensation, for these are equally affections of the subject of sensation.[2] Hence the terms in which we speak of sense-qualities have a two-fold meaning, for they are applicable primarily to the actual affections of the subject and secondarily to the affective qualities or powers of the external object which is the source of these affections.[3]

---

[1] *De Sensu et Sensibili*, vi, 446b.
[2] *Metaphysics*, Γ, v, 1010b. Cf. W. D. Ross's commentary *in loco*.
[3] *Categories*, viii, 9a–b.

## § 4

The mediaeval Aristotelians did not discuss any stage in the development of experience more primitive than the perception of the external world. Yet it is not without interest to note that Aquinas momentarily glances at the distinction between sensation and perception when, dealing with the veracity of the senses, he remarks that, although our judgments about external objects are fallible, we cannot be deceived in the awareness of the affection of sense which is no other than the sensation itself.[1]

When, in the seventeenth century, the criticism of experience became the central aim of philosophical inquiry, the subjectivity of sensation was at once acknowledged. Galileo pronounced for it, interpreting the external world in terms of quantitative characters. In the same way Descartes, beginning with the view that the contents of the mind were ideas purporting to represent external things, came in the end to the conclusion that there was no reason to believe that anything resembling sense-qualities existed in the external world. This is tantamount to saying that they are not really ideas or images at all but simply affections of the sentient subject.

Boyle distinguished quantitative characters as the primary modes or affections of matter from the secondary qualities, which correspond with the proper sensibles of Aristotle and exist not actually but only dispositively apart from sensation. Locke simplified, but perhaps did not improve, this terminology by speaking of the primary and secondary qualities; the primary qualities are, in fact, aspects of quantity, while the secondary qualities are the sense-qualities proper. Like Descartes, in declaring that the ideas of the secondary qualities

---

[1] St. Thomas Aquinas: *Summa Theologica*, I, qu. 17, art ii, ad 1m.

are not resemblances of external things, which only have the power of producing such ideas in our minds, Locke, in effect, retracts the application to them of the doctrine of representative ideas, and confesses that sense-qualities are real in their own right but belong to the sentient subject. In this connection he employs the argument, afterwards elaborated by Berkeley, that it is the same fire which produces in us the sensations of warmth and of pain. If, then, we do not suppose that the fire feels pain, it would be inconsistent to believe that it possesses the sense-quality of warmth.[1]

Berkeley, although still using the misleading word *idea*, has really overcome the erroneous presupposition of the doctrine of representative ideas. It is quite plain to him that sense-qualities do not even purport to belong to external objects, and he appeals simply to introspection for the evidence that they are affections of the sentient subject. His version of the pain argument is clearer than Locke's. It is that the sensation of heat and the feeling of pain when the heat is too great are the same thing. The heat itself as sensed is painful, not the awareness of it as an object. Hence the subject of the pain is himself the subject of the heat, or he would not feel pain[2].

The inadequacy of Berkeley's system is due, not to his correct assessment of the status of sensation, but to his attempt to reconstruct the whole universe out of minds and the sensations which are their contents. Hume, by abolishing unitary mind as well, makes the situation still more desperate. Reid, however, takes a much juster view, seeing not only where Berkeley was right but also where he was wrong. He congratulates Berkeley for "showing that the qualities of an inanimate thing, such as matter is conceived to be, cannot resemble any sensa-

[1] Locke: *Essay on the Human Understanding*, Bk. II, ch. viii, § 16.
[2] Berkeley: *Three Dialogues between Hylas and Philonous*, I (Campbell Fraser's ed., 1901, Vol. I, p. 385).

tion; that it is impossible to conceive anything like the sensations of our minds but the sensations of other minds".[1] But he does not regard the specific sense-qualities as the sole objects of which we are aware, and makes a respectable, if not completely satisfactory, attempt to provide an adequate criticism of experience. This was developed by his successors, and in particular by Hamilton. The recognition, however, of the subjectivity of sensation, which had been first expounded at length by Aristotle, was made by all these philosophers and may, therefore, be said to be very much of a common doctrine in classical European thought.

§ 5

The philosophy of the nineteenth century was dominated by Kantian phenomenalism, but in comparatively recent years there have been efforts from many directions to find a more promising approach to the criticism of experience and to treat the contents of sensation as real in their own right. The most familiar effort of this kind in our own country is the theory of sense-data, put forward by G. E. Moore and Bertrand Russell and developed by writers like C. D. Broad and H. H. Price. If enthusiasm for this theory has now waned, this is due to the attempt of its exponents to rebuild the world with too few bricks.

One defect has been the absence of any adequate view of the self as substance and agent and of its relation to sense-qualities. For some the self becomes a kind of disembodied awareness, having sense-data as its objects but in no way essentially connected with them, so that sense-data tend to take the place of the material world. For others the self is identical with its history; the series of sense-data takes the place of the self, and we are back in the position of Hume.

[1] Reid: *Inquiry into the Human Mind*, ch. V, sect. viii.

Another defect has been to suppose that we are aware of nothing but sense-data. Too many thinkers have tried to manufacture space and the external world out of sense-data, instead of frankly recognizing the subjectivity of sensation and looking beyond it for perceptual experience. The failure of so many enterprises of this sort has provoked a new scepticism about the foundations of knowledge. On the whole, sense-data have become awkward new entities, neither strictly material nor strictly mental, which get in the way of a satisfactory theory of either mind or matter.

G. E. Moore began bravely, in "The Refutation of Idealism", by asserting that sense-objects were presupposed to the awareness of them, and that there was no reason to believe that they could not exist without anyone being aware of them. Subsequent papers on "The Nature and Reality of Objects of Perception", "The Status of Sense-Data", and "Some Judgments of Perception",[1] represent a tenacious campaign to derive the material world from sense-data, either by establishing that sense-data themselves, or some of them, are parts of material objects or by finding some plausible relationship between sense-data and material objects. The thought which Moore expends on the former alternative shows in practice how highly sophisticated a so-called naïve realism would have to be. Moore confesses that he can arrive at no definite conclusion in either direction, and, if this is true of a thinker of Moore's calibre, it is a sign that his premises are inadequate. We are thereby confirmed in the opinion that we must begin by acknowledging not only the reality of sense-data but also their essential connection with the self, and must look elsewhere for the source of the perception of the external world.

While Moore has made a persistent although unsuccessful effort to do justice both to the self and to the material world, Russell has cheerfully sacrificed both,

[1] Collected in G. E. Moore: *Philosophical Studies.*

and left himself with sense-data alone. Originally, like Moore, he distinguished between the act of awareness and its object, but he came, later, to follow William James in denying the existence of consciousness as a distinctive type of entity. Hence sense-data become a neutral stuff which in one set of relations we call mind and in another we call matter. A mind is nothing but the sense-data and images which make up its history, while a material thing is a system of sense-data eked out with sensibilia, these latter being the sensations which would be experienced by an observer at points of view which, in fact, no observer occupies.[1] This, of course, is a return to Hume, and the first answer is that it does not in the least represent what we mean either by a mind or by a material thing. If it were true, it would be more accurate to say that neither minds nor material things exist, but only sense-data and images. The positive antidote is to recognize both the distinctive character of awareness and the existence of other objects of direct acquaintance in addition to sense-data.

§ 6

Meanwhile a theory of sense-data of the type proposed by Russell raises a point of interest, for it does have a meaning to speak of simply having a sensation as opposed to being aware of it. It is worth seeing what an experience on the level of bare sensation would be like. Any being which has sensations may also have images, which are intrinsically events of the same nature as sensations, although for the most part, as Hume remarks, but not universally, of less force and liveliness. We distinguish them by calling sensations those which we attribute to a new physical stimulation, while images

[1] Cf. B. Russell: *Analysis of Mind*, lect. I, V–VIII; *Our Knowledge of the External World*, lect. III–IV; and "The Relation of Sense-Data to Physics" in *Mysticism and Logic*.

are due to past sensations which they reproduce either with approximate exactitude or in fresh combinations. Thus we have the purely reproductive images of memory and the comparatively creative images of dream, fancy and aesthetic activity. It should be observed that the distinction between sensations and images is not as clearcut in application as it is in the abstract. Past experience is continually modifying what we should naturally call sensations. Consider the difference in our sensations when we enter a familiar room and when we enter an unfamiliar one; the filling out of the sensations in the former case by images of memory is easily recognizable upon reflection. In the same way, fancy is often an embroidery upon an actual sensation; on waking we may find that something, say the striking of a clock, which has played a part in a dream, is actually occurring. Hence, in practice, what we call a sensation is an event in which sensation in the strict abstract meaning of the term predominates, while an image is one in which imagery in the strict meaning predominates.

Thus, on the level of bare sensation, there is an experience which, although it does not resemble the external world, nevertheless corresponds in considerable detail with changes in the situation of the experient and in the external world. Think of the sensations, supplemented by images of memory, which you have when looking at any familiar object. Although they belong to you, and are, therefore, not really by themselves a perception of the external object as such, they might serve as a practical substitute for it and provoke appropriate behaviour. Hence a being on this level could be said by analogy to have an awareness of the external world, although it has no specific act of awareness in addition to its sensations. We may, indeed, believe that this is the kind of experience which animals have. It seems, then, that the more Humian sense-data theorists, in neglecting the distinctive nature of awareness proper and trying to explain perception in terms of combinations of sensations and images, have unwittingly made a valuable contribution to animal psychology.

Where they have erred is in supposing that human mind is confined to this level. For men, as we must acknowledge on reflection, not only have sensations but are in the proper sense aware of them. They are conscious that they have them; they judge that their experience exists. There enters a new factor, the factor of thought, of knowing or awareness in a specific sense. This ambiguity about awareness is of importance to observe. Primarily awareness means a distinctive cognitive act, whether of consciousness or of external perception or of abstract thinking, but it is often used also to designate the correspondence which obtains between sensation and the external world. The latter meaning is clearly different, derivative and analogical. In the discussion of sensation there has often been confusion about these two meanings of awareness. We find philosophers either treating sensation as if it were itself a department of thought with a specific cognitive act supervening upon the occurrence of the sense-quality, or else, in the somewhat grovelling manner of Hume and his followers, interpreting the whole development of human thought as merely a more and more elaborate construction of sensations and images.

On the level of bare sensation, then, we can speak of an awareness of the external world in a secondary and derivative meaning, but this is very different from a distinctive cognitive act, whether of consciousness or of external perception. To be conscious of a sensation is different from just having a sensation. To know in the full and proper sense what is other than oneself is not simply to possess a distorted reflection of it in oneself but to know it as it is in itself and as other than oneself. In the case of human thought it is a fatal error to stop with an account of sensations and images. We must, recognizing what genuine knowledge is, consider what

other factors besides sensation enter into our consciousness or immediate awareness of the present self, and go
on to discuss the perception of the external world without supposing that it is merely an elaboration of sensations and images.

## CHAPTER III

# CONSCIOUSNESS OF THE BODY

## § 1

THAT the specific sense-qualities, the secondary qualities or proper sensibles, belong to the sentient subject, and are objects of consciousness to a thinking mind, is evident upon reflection, and is fairly common doctrine among philosophers. We shall continue to call the carpet red, of course, but we can acknowledge without difficulty that this is to be understood causally. The carpet is such that, under the appropriate conditions of light and with normal eyesight, it stimulates a sensation of red.

This, however, presupposes the existence of that material object which is the carpet, and we have not yet examined the way in which we arrive at a knowledge of the material world. A material thing is essentially a mass extended in three dimensions. Hence we must inquire into the origin of spatial presentations, the source of the awareness of volumes. The importance of the discussion of the primary qualities or common sensibles is just that they are the fundamental characters of a body.

Some thinkers have maintained that spatial extension is to be found among the contents of sensation in exactly the same way as the proper sensibles. Several possibilities then present themselves. If the proper sensibles, or qualities like them, could be held to belong to material things, the same could be asserted of spatial characters; but, although we have not yet formally excluded the hypothesis that material things possess qualities resembling the proper sensibles, the suggestion does not appear, at first sight, very plausible. Perhaps special reasons could be discovered for attributing spatial characters to material things. Otherwise we should be left with volumes as transient ingredients of sensation, and it is difficult to see what the conception of the material world would be.

It could hardly be asserted that all sensations have contents extended in three dimensions. Sounds, smells, tastes and temperatures are clearly not voluminous. There remain sight and touch, and these senses have often been invoked for the origin of spatial notions. Aristotle himself, after saying that the apprehension of the common sensibles is due to movement, singles out sight and touch as operative in the awareness of movement.[1] This should, however, be interpreted without prejudice to Aristotle's familiar doctrine that spatial characters are really common sensibles, belonging to the sensibility as a whole rather than to any special sense. Accordingly it is only reasonable to suppose that he meant to assign a chief, rather than an exclusive, importance to sight and touch in the awareness of movement and of spatial characters in general. Nor is this out of harmony with our mature experience. We do, in fact, rely largely upon sight and touch for our judgments about spatial relations. The question of origin, nevertheless, remains to be solved. Whence do we first draw the notion of spatial extension? Are the sense-qualities of sight and touch themselves extended in three dimensions?

Locke seems to feel no difficulty in giving an affirmative answer. He declares it to be evident that we receive the simple idea of space from sight and touch.[2] On this supposition it is of interest to see why he holds that the ideas of the primary qualities resemble external reality, while the ideas of the secondary qualities are not resemblances. The reason he gives is disappointing. He says merely that spatial characters essentially belong to bodies, whereas the secondary qualities have no such connection with the idea of body. This is a little

---

[1] Aristotle: *De Anima*, II, vi, 418a.
[2] Locke: *Essay on the Human Understanding*, Bk. II, ch. v. and ch. xiii, § 2.

like saying that something is so because it would be extremely awkward if it were not. Locke has, however, a more plausible route to the external world by way of the experience of solidity and resistance, so that his system is not quite so fragile as his arguments about ideas would suggest. But the point at present is whether, as he asserts, visual and tactile data are themselves extended in space.

In our own day Locke's assertion finds an echo in the theory advanced by H. H. Price in his book on *Perception*. Price maintains that all visual sense-data possess depth or outness, and sensibly face in a certain direction. These factors, he declares after the manner of Locke, are just as much given as colour or shape. Within certain narrow limits visual data display perfect stereoscopy, so that their exact spatial relations are given; beyond this there is imperfect stereoscopy fading into the apparent flatness of distant visual data. Price asserts that tactile data, too, are often sensibly three-dimensional, and that they may be sensibly coincident with visual data belonging to the same external object.[1]

Berkeley's criticism of Locke in the *New Theory of Vision* is here very much to the point. Berkeley maintains that visual extension is in two dimensions only, and that distance, being, as he quaintly but graphically puts it, "a line directed endwise to the eye",[2] cannot be an immediate object of vision. He concedes to touch a certain experience of extension, but asserts that tactile extension is entirely distinct from visual extension. Visual extension is proper to sight and has the same subjectivity as light and colour; tactile extension is proper to touch and has the same subjectivity as tactile feeling. Berkeley admits no other experience of extension, and regards a material thing as nothing more than a bundle of the sense-qualities which are said to belong to it; his denial of the existence of material substance

---

[1] H. H. Price: *Perception*, pp. 217–223, 244–246.
[2] Berkeley: *New Theory of Vision*, § 2.

logically follows. Minds and their contents alone exist.

It is not our business now to pursue him in these latter assumptions and their consequences; we have only to consider his view of extension. On reflection he seems to be clearly right in holding that there is no extension which is common to sensations of sight and of touch. When, in the language of common sense, we speak of seeing and touching the same thing, a little thought will soon convince us that our experience is a good deal more complex than common sense would suggest. The immediate visual and tactile data, as we examine them in consciousness, are completely disparate; there is no identical element belonging to both.

In fact we may go further than Berkeley and assert that tactile data are not in themselves extended at all. When in thought we isolate the actual feelings of touch and consider them apart from their normal associations, it becomes absurd to speak of a larger or smaller tactile feeling. We associate them, of course, with larger or smaller parts of our own organisms or of external objects, but this is plainly a matter of association and not of the sense-datum in itself. Tactile data are no more extended than sounds, tastes, smells or temperatures.

The datum of vision, on the other hand, is certainly extended, but its extension is, as Berkeley says, in two dimensions, and must not be confused with spatial extension in three dimensions. Making once again the effort to consider the datum in itself and apart from its common-sense associations, we find that the visual datum is not at any distance from ourselves. Still less are different parts of it at different distances from us. It is flat, and a flat pictorial representation of ideal accuracy would give us precisely the same visual datum as a set of real bodies in three dimensions. The visual datum cannot strictly be called even a flat *surface*, for a surface is the surface of a volume, and there is no question of a third dimension, either given or implied, in the datum itself. The relating of it to the external world, and of different parts of it to external objects at different distances is plainly an interpretation which goes beyond what is presented in the datum itself.

Nor can the notion of volume be in any way manufactured out of sense-data. It might be vaguely supposed that the experience of movement led us to add a third dimension to visual data, and so to arrive at the conception of space. But, in the first place, the appreciation of local movement as such presupposes an awareness of space; without this it would be merely a change of sensations. Secondly, the notion of volume is not a complex construction due to bringing three dimensions together; it is an elementary notion which turns out to be capable of analysis in terms of three dimensions. The extension of a body is essentially in three dimensions given together as a whole, and in the material world a surface in two dimensions is merely an abstraction. Visual extension, on the other hand, is a concrete whole in two dimensions; a third dimension is alien to its nature. Hence there is positive opposition between the extension of the field of vision and the extension of a body. It follows not only that spatial extension is not given in the visual datum but that it cannot even be elaborated from it. For the source of spatial presentations we must look not to the qualities of sensation but to a distinct and primitive experience of voluminousness.

§ 2

Reid saw clearly the truth that sensation does not, by itself, account for the perception of bodies in space, but he was wholly at a loss to offer any explanation of how we arrive at the perception of an external spatial world. It is suggested to us, he says, on the occasion of sensation, primarily in connection with sensations of touch, but in a less perfect way also in connection with sight. It belongs to the original constitution of our nature both that we should conceive a spatial world and that we should believe that real bodies exist corresponding with our conceptions. Nevertheless, since bodies bear no resemblance to the sensations in connection with which we perceive them, their perception remains mysterious. For Reid, in short, the perception of a spatial world is just brute fact. It would be difficult to stay content with so summary a doctrine.[1]

If, indeed, we could make the notion of a spatial world no more intelligible than this, if there were a sudden jump from a medley of sensations to an ordered world of bodies, we might be tempted to fall into the arms of Kant and to regard the framework of space as the product of our own minds. In the relatively brief section on space at the beginning of the *Critique of Pure Reason* Kant asserts that we could not relate our sensations to anything outside ourselves, or be aware of them as not merely distinct but spatially ordered, unless the notion of space were already present to our minds. Hence the form of space is presupposed to experience; it is not empirical but belongs to the native furniture of the mind.

Kant is evidently assuming that the notion of space which he has to explain is that of external space, the space to which we relate our sensations, especially those of vision. He is assuming, also, that we necessarily regard sense-qualities as belonging to external things, and not merely as due to stimulation from them. This being so, he finds, upon reflection, that sensations are not in themselves spatially ordered, and do not of themselves point to an external object. Hence he concludes that it is the mind which spins the form of space out of itself and, by inserting sense-qualities into a spatial framework, turns sensations into objects. It follows that our spatial experience is not a knowledge of things as they are in themselves.

[1] Cf. Reid: *Inquiry into the Human Mind*, ch. v-vi, and *Essays on the Intellectual Powers*, essay II.

Kant is, in fact, making two hasty assumptions. He has not explored the possibility that the origin of spatial notions is to be found in the consciousness of our own bodies. Nor has he made the fairly obvious analysis of sensation which reveals that we are not bound to attribute sense-qualities to material objects in any but a causal relation. While sense-qualities remain genuine objects within the consciousness of the self, it is only by a confusion of thought that we may come to suppose that material things actually possess them. Why he was able to make these assumptions so easily becomes evident when we discover what his conception of space was. This appears when we examine his arguments in detail.

Space, he says, is given as a single, infinite whole; particular spaces can be conceived only as parts of this already given whole; and you can think away the existence of spatial objects, but you can never think away space itself. Hence the notion of space is necessary, independent of experience and presupposed to it.

If this is really the primitive notion of space, it certainly cannot be of empirical origin, but we need not admit too readily that we must think of space at once in this way. If we cast our minds back among Kant's predecessors, we begin to see what this notion of space is and where he got it. For it is Newton's conception of a uniform infinite space within which things exist and which is ultimately resolvable into the immensity of God. Its previous ancestry can be traced back to Gassendi and, through him, to the void of Leucippus and the ancient atomists.

> *Nam corpora sunt et inane,*
> *Haec in quo sita sunt et qua diversa moventur.*[1]

Kant does not name Newton in this connection, but he implicitly criticizes him without naming him. His criti-

[1] Lucretius: *De Rerum Natura*, I, 420-1.

cism is directed not towards Newton's conceiving space in this way, but only towards his regarding space thus conceived as a reality and not as the form of outer sensibility.[1]

Newton, however, was not so great a philosopher as he was a physicist, and Kant ought to have been much more critical of his incursions into the philosophical sphere. The notion of infinite space cannot be so easily taken for granted. On reflection it turns out not to be something given and complete at all; it is a notion always in the making. What we call infinite space is, in fact, only the indefinite extension of a finite space. Nor is empty space self-explanatory; it becomes intelligible only as the field of possibility of corporeal things. Hence the notion of finite and occupied space is primary. The primitive spatial presentation is of a finite body, and infinite empty space is merely an ideal construction relative to this.

One of the lines of thought to be found in Kant has, however, a certain initial plausibility. He claims that finite spaces cannot be conceived except as parts of infinite space, so that the notion of the latter is presupposed to them. The point of this argument becomes clearer in the *Antinomies* than it was in the *Transcendental Aesthetic*. What it amounts to is this. A finite space is a bounded space. But a space can appear as bounded only in relation to a space outside it. If that space is itself bounded, the same necessity recurs. Hence, in the end, you cannot conceive a finite space except in relation to infinite space outside it. The notion of infinite space is therefore primitive.

It is perfectly true, of course, that the notion of a boundary presupposes the recognition of at least the possibility of something outside it. So it truly follows that the primitive presentation of space cannot have definite boundaries. But it would be an error to con-

---

[1] Kant: *Kritik der reinen Vernunft*, "Allgemeine Anmerkungen zur transzendentalen Ästhetik", B 69–72.

clude that it must then be positively unbounded or infinite. All that logically follows is that its boundaries are not apprehended as such; it does not follow that it has no boundaries. The first confused notion of space may well be of a volume which is in fact finite but whose boundaries are not explicitly cognized. If, as we have maintained, infinite space cannot be a primitive notion, this must be so.

Yet to suppose a primitive awareness of a finite space of whose boundaries we are not yet explicitly aware presents a certain difficulty to the imagination which helps to explain why the origin of spatial notions has remained a somewhat obscure question. We have still to see what in the concrete is the scope of this awareness, but meanwhile the abstract conception may be made more intelligible by an example. For the field of vision is certainly finite, but we are not primitively aware of its boundaries; it may even give us a moment's trouble to acknowledge that it has boundaries. The reason is that we cannot see its boundaries; to claim to do so would involve a contradiction, for it would have to be true both that they were the boundaries of the field of vision and that we could see beyond them. As with the field of vision, so with the awareness of volumes, it may well be that we are primitively aware of an extension as such before we are aware of its boundaries as such.

Kant, therefore, does not succeed in demonstrating that infinite empty space is given as a presupposition of experience. It appears, on the contrary, to be an ideal construction based upon an experience of finite volumes. The Kantian view becomes attractive only if there is no means of bridging the gap between the medley of sensations and the conception of an ordered external spatial world. The natural direction in which to look for a solution of the problem would now appear to be in the consciousness of the bodily organism.

## § 3

Philosophers have, on the whole, neglected to explore the significance of the consciousness of the body, but Hamilton is an honourable exception. Unduly impressed by Kant's reasoning, he was ready to admit that the notion of space was a form of thought native to the mind, but he managed to combine with this opinion the assertion of an empirical acquaintance with spatial extension as an element in real things. We need not here consider the consistency of these two views, but can confine ourselves to the empirical side of his teaching. In his earlier *Lectures on Metaphysics*[1] he was still employing the common expedient of looking to vision for the origin of the experience of extension, but, when he came to edit Reid, he had acquired a more original point of view.

In his dissertations on Reid, Hamilton states that "the primary qualities are perceived as in our organism",[2] and that "all sensations, whatsoever, of which we are conscious, as one out of another, *eo ipso*, afford us the condition of immediately and necessarily apprehending extension; for in the consciousness itself of such reciprocal outness is actually involved a perception of difference of place in space and, consequently, of the extended":[3] As an attempt to scrutinize internal experience for the origin of spatial notions, this is an advance on Hamilton's earlier view, and on the views of his predecessors, but it can hardly be regarded as finally satisfactory. For sensations cannot be said in themselves to occupy space, and, while we recognize that different sensations which we have at the same time are distinct, it is not literally true that there is a distance between them. Hamilton, in tracing the original

[1] Sir William Hamilton: *Lectures on Metaphysics*, lect. xxviii.
[2] Hamilton's *Reid*, Note D*, p. 881.
[3] *Op. cit.*, Note D, p. 861 n.

experience of spatial extension to a relation between sensations, acknowledges that they do not in themselves occupy space. Yet his theory requires that they should be definitely localized; presumably, therefore, they are localized at points. But a mathematical point is not a part of space, and no real thing can be localized at a point. Hence we could apprehend a spatial relation between sensations only if they in themselves occupied space. This, however, is clearly erroneous.

Moreover, Hamilton asks us to find the origin of spatial notions in the experience of a spatial relation which is barely a fact of extension. But bare extension is not real and cannot be an object of experience. Just as real time is the duration of something, so real space is the extension of something. When we once have the notion of extension, we can isolate spatial relations, but if we derive it from experience, we must derive it from the experience of an extended thing. In other words, what we have to look for is an experience of body, not of a mere volume but of a mass, a volume with density.

It is the merit of Locke to have made this clear in his criticism of the Cartesians. Physics is evidently not a branch of pure mathematics. Yet the truth that progress in the physical sciences is due to the application of mathematical methods has at various times, not excluding our own, brought with it a tendency to minimize those non-mathematical factors in physics to which the mathematical methods are applied. The physics of Descartes was a geometer's physics, taking explicit account of nothing save extension and motion. Locke points out, in opposition, the distinction between extension and what he calls solidity. That he describes solidity as an idea of touch, as if it were merely a tactile quality, is a mistake which does not detract from the value of the rest of what he has to say about it.

Solidity, for Locke, is the property of occupying space, from which follows the power of resistance to bodies outside; this in no wise follows from mere extension.[1] Locke's philosophy is here in harmony with the physics of his contemporary, Newton, for whom the fundamental conception of matter is derived not from volume alone but from volume and density, whose product is mass. Reid repeats Locke's distinction without doing full justice to its significance, but Hamilton himself, in an abstract discussion of the primary qualities, is quite clear in deriving them from the twin roots of extension and solidity, the latter being equivalent to ultimate incompressibility.[2]

It is, indeed, evident on reflection that a geometrical world of pure extension is only an abstraction, a phantom and not a reality. Pure extension cannot move. When a thing moves, its former position in space remains where it was, but it is obviously not an independent reality. Real extension in three dimensions belongs to a mass, a volume with solidity or density. Any attempt by the too mathematically-minded physicist to get rid of real extended things would simply leave him with space as real, and space, in order to be real, would have to possess density. Hence what we are looking for at present is not a bare experience of the voluminousness of our bodies but an experience of our bodies as masses. Too many thinkers have tried to find the primitive awareness of spatial facts in an abstract apprehension of purely geometrical properties. When we have avoided this error, we are on the way to a satisfactory theory.

§ 4

The consciousness of ourselves as embodied is usually associated with general or organic sensation, with that vague background of experience, sometimes rising to stronger pleasures or sharper pains, which serves to

[1] Locke: *Essay on the Human Understanding*, Bk. II, ch. iv and xiii.
[2] Sir W. Hamilton: *Lectures on Metaphysics*, lect. xxiv.

inform us of the condition of various parts of the organism. But it is still true of these feelings, as of all sensations, that they are not in themselves voluminous. The feelings themselves are no more extended in three dimensions than are the data of sight, hearing, taste, smell and touch. Nevertheless, the customary reference to them for the experience of the self as embodied is justified in so far as the consciousness of a mass connected with them is normally clearer than it is with those sensations whose import for common sense is primarily external.

For, when we have a feeling, as we say, in the head or arms or any other part of the body, we are unmistakably conscious not only of the feeling itself but also of a region of the body, whether larger or smaller, connected with it. A feeling of temperature, of warmth or cold, is as good an example as any organic sensation. A feeling of warmth, say, is more or less intense, but it is not in itself extended. If we confine our attention to the mere sensations, we are not immediately aware of a distance between the sensation of warmth in one part of the body and the sensation of cold in another when we are sitting in front of a fire with our backs exposed to a draught. Yet, even when the intensity of the sensation is the same, there is a quantitative difference between the warmth of my finger held near a candle-flame and the warmth of my whole body in front of a fire. This difference, while it is not a difference of volume in the sensations themselves, which are not voluminous, we can recognize, on reflection, to be due to a difference of volume in the regions connected with these sensations. This latter difference of volume, when we are conscious of the sensations, also naturally rises to consciousness. Thus, too, when we feel a sensation of warmth or cold spreading over the body, the interpretation of this experience, while it is not that the sense-quality itself is becoming more voluminous, is truly that a progressively larger region of the body is connected with the sense-quality.

It is plain that this primitive consciousness of mass, as we reflect on it in itself, is much less clearly defined than our developed spatial notions. The reason is that it has not yet been symbolized in visual terms. Although the visual datum has only two dimensions, it is admirably adapted for the definition and comparison of different areas, and we all naturally and spontaneously employ a visual symbolism for the clarification of spatial notions. Our geometry, while it is not strictly a geometry of visibles, since it deals with lines and points, which are invisible, is nevertheless a geometry based on thought about visibles, and it could not be as exact as it is if we had no visual symbolism of which to avail ourselves.

The direct consciousness of the body, however, as we saw when dealing with Kant that it must be, and as on reflection it actually turns out to be, is a consciousness of finite masses, vaguely larger or smaller, but without any defined boundary. We can be explicitly aware of limits only when we are aware of at least the possibility of something outside them. Hence we become aware of the limits of the body only when we begin to be aware of the external world, and we become aware of the limits of one part of the body in relation to another only when we begin to be aware of that other part in the same manner as we perceive the external world. This would carry us beyond the stage of discussion which we have at present reached. Here we are concerned with something psychologically more primitive, with the purely internal consciousness of a mass whose parts and limits have not yet been explored. Yet we could not acquire the outward-looking apprehension of the boundaries of a mass unless we had an internal apprehension of the mass simply as mass.

The difference between the primitive consciousness of the body and the later visual symbolism of its spatial character also provides an explanation of errors of localization. In the classical example of the man who thinks that he feels pain in a foot which has in fact been amputated, we have not to admit that his consciousness deceives him. His original consciousness of the pain as belonging to a region of the body is, as consciousness must be, infallible, but, in attributing it to the foot, he is referring it to his customary visual picture of the body, and his correlation of the datum with the image is inefficient and leads him astray.

If this is a correct view of the consciousness of body, it is not difficult to see that it accompanies the consciousness not only of organic sensations and of feelings of temperature but also of every other kind of sensation. This will probably be admitted readily enough in the case of cutaneous sensations of touch, and it should on reflection, be admitted also in respect of sight and hearing, taste and smell. With these latter senses the extent of the body affected varies so little, and the attention so tends to be concentrated on their external significance, that we might overlook the bodily consciousness accompanying them, but it is undoubtedly discoverable if we care to reflect. Hence there is justification for Aristotle's description of extension and its modes as common sensibles.

Consciousness of the body accompanies consciousness of sensation and does not occur apart from sensation. Since it is a consciousness of the part of the body connected with sensation, it is not a consciousness of the body as a whole, nor is it a steady consciousness of any one part of it. Sensation first arouses consciousness, and consciousness then redounds upon the part of the organism connected with the sensation. This appears to be a secure deliverance of reflection, and it explains both why some hasty thinkers have recognized nothing in consciousness except sensation, and why it is useless to try to divert the attention from sensation in order to have an exclusive consciousness of the body. The self as embodied must be seized by consciousness in connection with the self as sensing.

So far we have spoken vaguely of the part of the body

connected with sensation. In what does this connection consist? It seems evident, on reflection, that the part of the body of which we become conscious in connection with sensation is the part in which mechanical changes transmit the stimulus to sensation. The object of consciousness is a part of the body in a state of mechanical tension, of stress and strain. Without these changes the material organism would not rise to consciousness, and it is because these changes stimulate a sensation that the consciousness of the sensation redounds upon the part of the body whose mechanical activity provides the requisite stimulus.

While sensations are not in themselves spatially extended, they manifest a difference of modality in accordance with the greater or lesser volume to which, in this way, they belong. Hence it is not without reason that Ward, for example, speaks of all sensations as having intensity, protensity or duration, and extensity.[1] Extensity, however, as Ward himself acknowledges, must be understood in a rather different way from the two other quantitative attributes. In accordance with the foregoing exposition we must say that, while every sensation has in itself a determinate intensity and a determinate duration, it has not in itself a determinate spatial extension, but only a definite modality as connected with a determinate volume. In this way we might distinguish the extensity of all sensations both from the two-dimensional extension of visual data and from the three-dimensional extension of bodies.

It may be useful to sum up this discussion. The factor of volume, which is essential to the notion of the material world, is not to be found in mere sensation. Although sensations, especially those of sight and touch, are closely associated with the exploration of space, no sensation is in itself voluminous. But there is no reason to believe that space is a form contributed by our own minds to the constitution of objects. We are not obliged

[1] J. Ward: *Psychological Principles*, ch. v, § 2, 2nd ed. 1920, p. 105.

to think that the original presentation is of infinite space; it may well be of a finite space, although, since by hypothesis we are as yet aware of nothing beyond it, we are not aware of its boundaries as such. We should, however, go astray if we looked for an experience of pure volume, for pure volume is a geometrical abstraction. Real volume is volume with density, or mass. Do we then have a primitive experience of finite mass? The answer is to be found in the consciousness of the body. We are not conscious of the body except when also conscious of a sensation, but, when we are conscious of a sensation, we are conscious as well of the part of the body whose properly corporeal or mechanical activity transmits the stimulus. This experience is the source of spatial notions.

## CHAPTER IV

# EXPERIENCE OF DURATION

§ 1

ALTHOUGH considerable difficulties are presented by the place of temporal factors in experience, time is not as perplexing as space. We have to find the origin of spatial notions in a consciousness of mass which occurs only in connection with sensation and is liable to be obscured in reflection by the comparative liveliness of the sense-qualities which it accompanies. Materiality, we must acknowledge, is of all the elements of experience the farthest removed from essential intelligibility. A temporal character, on the other hand, belongs to all the factors of experience, so that, although time has difficulties of its own as well as others in common with space, we can find and fix its notion more readily.

Kant claims to establish the subjectivity of time on grounds parallel to those which he alleges in respect of space. They admit of similar answers. We could not, he says, become aware of sensations as temporally ordered unless the notion of time were already in our possession. This appears to suppose that time consists essentially in an order or series of relations, and that a single sensation does not in itself have duration. Not only is this a rash supposition but reflection on experience plainly contradicts it.

As in the question of space, Kant's other reasoning shows why he was so hasty in denying the empirical origin of the notion of time. Time, he asserts, is given as a single, infinite whole; particular times can be conceived only as parts of this already given whole; and you can think away the existence of temporal objects, but you can never think away time itself. Hence the form of time, like that of space, is necessary, independent of experience and presupposed to it.

But, as with infinite space, so we must say of infinite time that it is not a complete given whole but a notion always in the making; it is an indefinite extension of a finite time. Empty time is as much an ideal construction as empty space; real time is the duration of real temporal things. Once again it is the absolute time of Newton which Kant assumes to be a primitive and self-explanatory notion, and which he merely transmutes from the reality which it was for Newton into the form of inner sensibility which it is for himself. In fact his assumption is unjustifiable; the ideal conception of infinite time demands to be derived from finite time, and not finite time from infinite time.

We saw that the most substantial difficulty against the primitive spatial experience being of a finite volume was that its limits could not be recognized unless we were aware of a space outside it. A similar difficulty can be raised about time, and can be answered in the same way. If to be aware of a finite time entailed being explicitly aware of its limits, this must include an awareness of a time outside it. Either this time outside it is itself finite or not. If it is finite, the same consequence recurs. Hence, if awareness of a finite time entails an explicit awareness of its limits, it must in the end presuppose the notion of infinite time. It is, however, gratuitous to assume that an experience of what is in fact a finite duration is impossible without an explicit awareness of the limits which make it finite. Consequently, we are still entitled to look for a primitive experience of finite duration which does not include an explicit awareness of its limits. In short, Kant's attempted demonstration of the subjectivity of time fails for the same reasons as his parallel effort with space, and the inquiry for an empirical origin of temporal notions is still open.

§ 2

There is evidently a close association between the notion of time and that of change. While a temporal being is not necessarily the subject of continuous change, it must, nevertheless, be continuously changeable. An unchangeable being is not spread out in duration, is not temporal, and thereby differs from any changeable being, even from one which never ceases to exist. To adopt the distinction of Boethius, an indefinitely extended duration may be called perpetuity, but eternity in the strict sense, excluding the possibility of change, transcends what we know as duration by a positive perfection beyond our conception.[1]

If time is thus bound up with changeability, it presents a special difficulty from which the notion of space is exempt. For all the potential parts of a volume exist simultaneously, and, although a volume is, absolutely speaking, infinitely divisible, it is not infinitely divided. We do not have to suppose that it actually possesses an infinite multitude of parts. But the parts of time exist one after another, and, in any finite time, we can distinguish a part which is before and a part which is after. It might seem that time was not only infinitely divisible but infinitely divided, and that any finite time consisted of an actually infinite multitude of successive moments.

It is this feature of time which, much more than the infinite divisibility of space, lends colour to the celebrated paradoxes of Zeno. An arrow in flight is, nevertheless, at any given moment at rest. For at any indivisible moment it simply occupies a single place, and that is to be at rest. Achilles, pursuing the tortoise, does not reach the tortoise's initial position until the reptile is some distance ahead. When he reaches the second position of the tortoise, the reptile has already progressed a little farther, and so on *ad infinitum*. Hence he

[1] Boethius: *De Consolatione Philosophiae*, lib. V, pr. 6.

61

cannot in a finite time overtake the tortoise. The paradoxes depend on the supposition that space and time
have an infinite multitude of parts; possibly Zeno intended to cast ridicule on this supposition. While it is
comparatively easy to see that space is infinitely divisible
but not infinitely divided, it is not quite so easy to see
this of time. If no two parts of time co-exist, how can
they not be actually distinct one from the other? And,
if they are, will not time consist of an infinite multitude
of indivisible moments?

One way out of this difficulty is to take the bold course
of denying the infinite divisibility of time and asserting
instead that any stretch of time consists of a finite number
of successive unit moments. Thus time becomes assimilated to number rather than to linear extension. This
was the solution of Berkeley and Hume. Locke had
derived the notion of time from the observation of ideas
succeeding one another in the mind, followed by the
recognition of a distance between their successive appearances.[1] Berkeley frankly confesses that his reflection
attained nothing but the succession of ideas; the conception of an infinitely divisible distance between them
seemed to him to be a myth. "Time, therefore, being
nothing, abstracted from the succession of ideas in
our minds, it follows that the duration of any finite
spirit must be estimated by the number of ideas or
actions succeeding each other in that same spirit or
mind."[2]

Hume develops a similar doctrine at greater length.[3]
He rashly asserts in general that nothing can be infinitely divisible without actually possessing an infinite
multitude of parts. This confusion of divisibility with
division is easily seen to be an error, but Hume notices
that his contention acquires additional force, or, as we
should say, sole plausibility, in the case of time.

---

[1] Locke: *Essay on the Human Understanding*, Bk. II, ch. xiv.
[2] Berkeley: *Principles of Human Knowledge*, § 98.
[3] Hume: *Treatise of Human Nature*, Bk. I, part II, esp. sect. i–iii.

"For the same reason, that the year 1737 cannot concur with the present year 1738, every moment must be distinct from, and posterior or antecedent to another. 'Tis certain then, that time, as it exists, must be compos'd of indivisible moments. For if in time we could never arrive at an end of division, and if each moment, as it succeeds another, were not perfectly single and indivisible, there would be an infinite number of co-existent moments, or parts of time; which I believe will be allow'd to be an arrant contradiction."[1]

Hume concludes that, since the mind is incapable of a positive conception of an infinite multitude, the conception of the duration of anything must be of a finite series of indivisible moments, time being constituted by the relations of succession between them.

This solution is not as intellectually satisfying as it is courageous. Hume, of course, confused thought with imagination, and proceeded as if what could not be imagined could not be thought. When, however, we really think about time, it is just evident that, with whatever speed one event may succeed another, we can always conceive the possibility that it should have succeeded more quickly. This means that the event gave rise to a state which, however fleeting, possessed a finite duration than which a shorter duration can always be conceived. It follows that time does not consist exclusively of relations of succession; the succession is a succession of durations, and these durations are infinitely divisible.

Locke, therefore, was right in requiring duration as well as succession, but his account of the origin of the notion of time is open to objection in other respects. Reid criticizes him acutely for putting the observation of succession first and that of duration afterwards.[2] If the ideas whose succession we observe had themselves

[1] *Loc. cit.*, sect. ii (ed. Selby-Bigge, p. 31).
[2] Reid: *Essays on the Intellectual Powers*, essay III, ch. v.

no duration, the duration between them would be a duration of nothing. Reality would belong only to the points in time at which events occurred, but points are not parts of an extension, and so time would, in fact, disappear. Time would be a void, and things would be timeless. Real duration cannot be merely a distance between events, but must be the intrinsic duration of real temporal things. Consequently Reid denies Locke's assertion that no duration can be observed where there is no actual change.

Reid, however, in expounding his own theory of time, asserts that an awareness of duration necessarily includes past as well as present; hence he ascribes the awareness of duration to memory.[1] To ascribe an original awareness to memory is contrary to the usual view of the purely repetitive character of that function of mind, and should not be admitted without scrutiny. What Reid is presupposing is the knife-edge view of the now, the belief that the real present moment is an indivisible point in time. This seems at first sight natural enough, and it has been a persistent belief, but it demands further examination.

§ 3

The attempt made by Berkeley and Hume to interpret time in terms of number is, then, incompatible with time as experienced. Time is the field of continuous changeability and, as such, must be assimilated to linear extension rather than to number. But, if we press the literal application of this image of time as a linear dimension, it would seem that the present moment, the now, can be represented only by a point moving along it. These, at any rate, are the conceptions of time and of the now which have been firmly entrenched in classical physics since Galileo. The absolute time of Newton confers reality upon this linear dimension,

[1] *Loc. cit.*, ch. iii.

regarded as actually infinite and ultimately reducible to the divine eternity. As, however, we suggested in dealing with space, we need not pay the same respect to Newton's philosophical excursions as we do to his strictly physical work. We want to see what precisely is the relation of the linear image of time to time as experienced, and it may not turn out to be so simple a correspondence as Newton supposed. As a matter of fact the notion of now as a point in the linear dimension of time is a good deal older than modern physics, and was causing perplexity to thinkers at earlier periods. It is the root of the difficulties which Augustine felt, and so vividly expressed in his justly celebrated discussion of time in the *Confessions*.[1]

Augustine is quite clear that time is real only with the existence of temporal or changing things. When no changing thing existed, it follows that there was no time. But time cannot be identified with the motion of any particular temporal things, say, of the heavenly bodies. For, if these ceased to exist, or ceased to move while other changing things continued to be, there would still be time. Hence, while the motion of the heavenly bodies affords a convenient measure of time, it is not itself time.

Augustine's difficulties really begin when he asks how we come to perceive and are able to measure time. We speak of a long or a short time, but these are in the past or the future, for the present is not a length of time. Past time, however, is no longer real, and future time is not yet real. We have in our minds images of the past and of the future, but these images will not by themselves serve as a basis for the measurement of time, for they are present. We should strictly say, not that there are three times, past, present and future, but that there was the past, there is the present and there will be the future.

The present being a point in time, how can we in the

[1] St. Augustine: *Confessions*, XI, 14-31.

present measure the past and the future, which are at present non-existent? We might say that we measure time as it is passing, but this is not really satisfactory. For we can measure a length only when it has a beginning and an end, and time as it is passing means a time which has not yet ended. Here Augustine seems to be trying to transcend the conception of the present as a point in time, but he is unable, in the end, to see how to do so. He has to say that time measured is remembered and prospective time, not merely their images but the times themselves as apprehended by a mind whose scope is not confined to the bare present. Like Reid long afterwards, he attributes the original awareness of time to memory. *Aliquid in memoria mea metior, quod infixum manet.*

## § 4

There can be no doubt that the chief difficulty about time arises from the conception of the real now as a point in time. Is this conception so obviously valid as it has been assumed to be? It is no doubt a serviceable abstraction for scientific purposes, but what is its value in terms of experience? For the real now for me is the time of my present experience, which really exists and is really distinct from my past and future experience. If this is a point in time, it follows that in any finite stretch of time there is an infinite multitude of such nows. In that case it is impossible to see how we could escape the paradoxes of Zeno. Russell has suggested that these are bogus difficulties which can be evaded by utilizing the notion of a compact series, that is, a series between any two members of which other members can always be found.[1] This is an interesting mathematical expedient, but it leaves the philosophical question untouched. For a compact series is not a series in the proper sense; it is just simply a continuum, and there is not a

[1] B. Russell: *Our Knowledge of the External World,* lect. v and vi.

genuine series unless there is discontinuity. The notion
of a compact series is, therefore, a way of assimilating a
continuum to a series, but it must not be taken to imply
that a continuum really is a series. Russell's suggestion
amounts only to a denial that points in time are real;
it does not tell us how to transcend the conception of
now as a point in time.

If we retain the conception of now as a point, we can
avoid the paradoxes of Zeno only by adopting the view
of Berkeley and Hume, and supposing that time is a
genuine discontinuous series of timeless points separated
by durations which are the durations of nothing. But
we have already noticed that this will not serve; real
duration is the duration of something, and mere duration is no more a reality than mere space. Moreover,
if the real now is a point in time, both our present awareness and its present object exist as such for no time.
How, then, can we say that they exist at all? From all
this it is plain that the conception of the real now as
a point in time leads us into insoluble difficulties.

The reason why this conception has been adopted is
that any duration contains parts which are before and
parts which are after; it cannot, therefore, be one present.
But the assumption of this argument is highly questionable. We must ask ourselves whether it is true that
every duration contains a real before and a real after.
No doubt, when we think of any stretch of time, its
parts are clearly marked off one from the other. When,
however, we think of a time during which no change
has occurred, it offers us no real before and after; we
can only insert before and after into it by supposing
possible changes which might have taken place. In
other words, there is no real before and after unless there
is real change; a stretch of duration within which no
change occurs is one in which, since changes might
occur, there are potentially earlier and later parts, but
there is no real division of earlier and later. Just as a
homogeneous volume is potentially divisible but actually

undivided, so a homogeneous duration is potentially divisible but actually undivided. The time in which anything endures unchanged remains a unity.

That which is a real unity is experienced as a unity. Hence the real now of experience is not a point in time but a finite duration, that stretch of time during which experience persists unchanged. This usually extremely brief stretch of time which is the real present must be distinguished from the specious present of the psychologist, which includes the very recent past from which elements have survived into the present in spite of changes in other objects of experience. The other now which is a point in time remains as a useful abstraction for scientific purposes, but it is not the real now of experience.

The primitive experience of time is, then, the unitary awareness of a duration within which experience persists unchanged. This duration is finite, but its limits are not explicitly apprehended until there is an apprehension of change, and this is impossible without memory. Nor do we distinguish in it what is before and what is after until we think of the changes which might have occurred in it. Nevertheless, this is in fact an experience of duration, and it is the foundation of our later and more complex notions of time.

Another conclusion remains to be drawn. This is that continuous change, while it presents an intelligible abstract. concept, is not a possible object of awareness in its concreteness. For continuous change has a duration which is pure flow without any pause at a real now. It never is; it is simply becoming. Awareness, on the other hand, is necessarily of something which is; it is essentially at a now, and a real now is a stretch of duration without change. When we say that a continuous motion has now reached such a stage, this now, being a point in time, is not a real now but an ideal construct imposed on fact by thought. It is a significant concept, having the basis in fact that the motion might stop at any point, but it is not a reality. When we observe what we take to be a continuous motion, there must be a rapid succession of acts of awareness like those which we presumably have when watching a cinematographic performance. That this succession of acts of awareness indicates a continuous motion in the object of which we are aware, is not a datum of experience but an interpretation of thought.

This conclusion is confirmed by two facts. The first is that there is no perceptible difference between what we call an observation of continuous change and our experiences at a picture theatre, although the latter are admittedly due to a rapid succession of still pictures. Secondly, we can reasonably discuss whether continuous change really occurs, but this would scarcely be a reasonable matter for discussion if it were given in experience. It is relevant to the criticism of Bergson to remark that, while the concrete awareness of consciousness and perception has a certain necessarily static character, abstract thought is precisely the function of mind which enables us to envisage the possibility of a pure becoming.

## § 5

It may be worth while to make a comparison and draw a parallel between the experience of voluminousness and the experience of duration. When we come to reflect upon our already acquired notions of space and time, it may be that we think first of infinite space as the receptacle of material things and of infinite time as the field of events. But it is not difficult to acknowledge that space and time in this sense are not real; reality belongs to the finite volumes and durations of real things. The empirical origin of spatial and temporal notions must be sought in an awareness of finite spaces and times.

Nor can we expect to find an awareness which is barely of space and time, for real extension belongs to an extended thing. What we are looking for is not an experience of voluminousness and duration by themselves but an experience of voluminous and enduring things. All the elements of our experience possess the character of duration, but, as far as spatial properties are concerned, this means that we are looking for an experience of mass.

We notice, too, that an explicit knowledge of the boundaries of an extension presupposes a knowledge of what is or may be outside it, so that we must expect the primitive awareness of mass and duration, although of finite mass and duration, to lack explicit delimitation. It will lack also the explicit recognition of parts, for a homogeneous extension has only potential and not actual parts, and can be thought of as having parts only by making the supposition of a division of the mass or of a change within the duration.

This being so, we find at last that we have a primitive awareness of volume in the consciousness of those parts of the body which transmit the stimulus of sensation. We find also that, however rapid the succession of elements in experience may be, these elements could not exist or be experienced unless they had some duration. A duration within which no change occurs is a unity, and is experienced as a unity. Thus we find in consciousness the primitive experiences of mass and of duration out of which our more elaborate notions of space and time are built.

## CHAPTER V

# THE SELF AS SUBSTANCE AND AGENT

## § 1

WE have been exploring the contents of consciousness, of the immediate awareness of the present self, but we have not yet touched on the question whether the self simply is its contents or there is at the same time an awareness of an essential self distinct from its acts and attributes. The problem of substance has received extremely cavalier treatment in modern times. The distinction of substance and attribute is often treated as prescientific mythology, yet it is firmly entrenched in the structure of language and in the plain man's thinking; at any rate it deserves a more extended and careful consideration than it in fact receives from many philosophers to-day.

The Cartesian *Cogito* sounds at first like a promising approach to the matter. I think, therefore I am; the awareness of a mental process entails the awareness of the self to which the process belongs. But to what precisely does the *Cogito* amount in the view of its author? In the first place, it must be defended against the charge that it is an inference, and, at its place in Descartes' system, a dubious inference. Gassendi objected that it was an argument presupposing the major premiss that whatever thinks, exists, a premiss which Descartes on his principles was not yet entitled to affirm. In his reply Descartes, while asserting the truth of this premiss, and admitting that it was in a certain sense implied by his line of thought, denied altogether that it had to be explicitly considered and asserted in the *Cogito* itself. In other words, the *Cogito* was intended as an elementary analysis of a particular fact; the self was to be discovered in its thinking.

In the *Discours de la Méthode* Descartes, enucleating the results of the *Cogito*, says quite simply that he thereby knew himself at once to be a substance whose nature was to think. In the *Metaphysical Meditations* he does not at this point introduce the notion of substance, but defers it until he has dealt with the existence of the material world. The reason for this is to be found in what he took substance to mean. He had derived this notion from the Aristotelian scholastic tradition, but not from the best sources of this tradition; he accepted it as he found it, and made no essential alteration, but his application of it shows how incomplete his understanding was. The notion he adopted was simply that of the independent existent, that which does not exist in anything else as in a subject. When he defines substance as that which does not require anything other than itself in order to exist, this would strictly apply only to God, and would seem to lead to the paradoxes of Spinoza, but Descartes corrects himself at once and says that substance is that which, in order to exist, requires only the ordinary concourse of God.

Nevertheless, when Descartes comes to apply this definition of substance, he arrives at conclusions very different from those of the scholastic tradition. Ideas can only be objects of thought, and so they are not substances. But Descartes can find no factor more fundamental than thinking itself; thinking, like extension, is the subject of numerous modifications, but, like extension too,[i] it does not appear itself to be a modification of anything. Hence thinking and extension are the primary substantial properties of mind and matter respectively. Matter is necessarily extended, and extension is its substance. Mind, likewise, is necessarily and continuously an activity of thinking: "It seems necessary that the mind should always actually think; for thought constitutes its essence, just as extension constitutes the essence of body, nor is it conceived as an attribute which can be present or absent, as in a body is conceived the division of parts or motion."[1] Thinking, then, is the very essence or substance of mind. Since thinking and extension both have this character of ultimacy, and since they are mutually independent in essence, mind and matter can be affirmed to be two distinct substances, although Descartes hastens to add that, in the case of man, they are so conjoined that they can in another and secondary sense be said to form one substance.

Consequently, when Hobbes objects to his hastily substantializing the notion of thought and Descartes replies by making the conventional distinction between the substance itself and its activity of thinking, it is difficult to see what this can really mean for him. The acid test is in the assertion that the mind always thinks. If Descartes maintains that the mind must always be actually thinking, it can only be because he holds that this actual thinking is the substance of mind. To what then does the *Cogito* come? It might seem that *I think, therefore I am* is merely equivalent to *I think, therefore I think*. But it is not really quite so banal as this. For by substantiality Descartes means at least reality; to be real is either to be a substance or to belong to a substance. Hence, on final analysis, the *Cogito* can best be paraphrased in this way: in the consciousness of thinking lies an immediate recognition of the reality of thought. This is just and true as far as it goes; it is the expression of an essential realism which has managed to survive in spite of the doctrine of representative ideas. Nevertheless it is not an assertion that there exists a subject of thinking distinct from the act of thought. On this point Descartes must be held to take the view that consciousness discovers nothing but the thinking itself and the ideas which are its objects.

[1] Descartes in a letter to Arnauld, 4 June, 1648.

§ 2

Locke retains the plain man's belief in some sub-stratum of acts and attributes, but evidently has no notion of what philosophical analysis to make of it. He delights in repeating that we have no positive idea of substance; it is simply an unknown somewhat which is the subject of qualities and activities. "It is but a supposed I-know-not-what, to support those ideas we call 'accidents'."[1] He professes himself to be hurt when the Bishop of Worcester suggests that this is tantamount to making away with the notion of substance, but so obscure a notion, if it really is so obscure, could hardly be worth preserving, and it is not easy to see what right Locke could have to be so sure of its validity if he was unable to glimpse it more distinctly.

Where Locke felt himself on firmer ground was in describing how, by finding groups of qualities in constant conjunction, we frame the complex idea of a substance to which these qualities belong. Hume took the obvious next step by reducing the notion of substance to the established association of the group of qualities which in common language we attribute to one thing. "A subject of inhesion to sustain and support them" was an "unintelligible chimera".[2] Kant, then, on his usual principle, conceded to Hume that the notion of substance could not be got out of the matter of experience, but, recognizing that it was natural and indispensable, maintained that it should be regarded as an *a priori* category of thought by which the mind represented objects to itself and made experience intelligible.

If no more could be said, this might well conclude an obituary notice of the concept of substance. On the general ground of the essential relationship of genuine knowledge to reality the Kantian principle is unaccept-

[1] Locke: *Essay on the Human Understanding*, Bk. II, ch. xxiii, § 15.
[2] Hume: *Treatise of Human Nature*, Bk. I, part iv, sect. iii (ed. Selby-Bigge, p. 222).

able; we should be left in the position of Hume, and should have to look upon substance as a notion which failed to survive exact philosophical analysis. There is, however, something more to say, and it is worth looking for the traces of a more adequate theory among the philosophers of modern times.

Reid criticizes Hume in terms which less exuberantly anticipate Bradley's delightful gibe at the Humian self as a collection of mutually cognizant onions on a non-existent rope.[1] He asks whether a succession of ideas and impressions may eat and drink and be merry, and whether ideas can remember impressions or impressions ideas. For Reid it is simply evident, and it would be irrational to deny, that there is a subject of thoughts and feelings and volitions. He clearly thinks that, more fortunate than Locke, he has a positive notion of what this subject is. When he contrasts it with its acts and attributes as the permanent with the transitory, his inspiration is scarcely happy, for, if substance is a real and distinct factor, there could presumably be a substance which endured for only a minimal length of time. The notion of a substance cannot be reduced to that of a continuant; we still want to know what sort of a reality it is which is such as to be a continuant, and that is to ask more fundamentally what substance is. But Reid is more convincing when he refers to substance as the subject of pleasure and pain, and distinguishes the self from its thoughts and volitions as the agent from its acts. He does not, however, develop this line of thought at length.[2]

Half a century earlier Berkeley had shown much more decision in distinguishing substance from attribute as the agent from its activity. His discussion of the knowledge which we have of spirit is well worth attention.[3]

[1] F. H. Bradley: *Ethical Studies*, essay I (2nd ed., pp. 33-40).
[2] Cf. Reid: *Essays on the Intellectual Powers*, essay I, ch. ii, essay III, ch. iv, and essay VI, ch. v.
[3] Berkeley: *Principles of Human Knowledge*, §§ 27 and 135-142.

Using *idea* in his characteristic manner as signifying sense-quality, he denies that we have an idea of spirit but holds that we have a perfectly clear awareness of it as instanced in our own minds. He had originally employed *idea* and *notion* as synonymous, but, in the second edition of the *Principles*, he finds it profitable to make a distinction and to state that we have a notion, though not an idea, of spirit. The difference arises from the essential passivity of ideas or sense-qualities, whereas the notion of spirit is an awareness of the agent which perceives, thinks and wills. "All the unthinking objects of the mind agree, in that they are entirely passive, and their existence consists only in being perceiv'd: whereas a soul or spirit is an active being, whose existence consists not in being perceiv'd, but in perceiving ideas and thinking."[1]

This sends our minds at once a generation farther back to Leibniz, with his emphatically dynamic conception of substance. In the *Système Nouveau de la Nature* Leibniz tells how, having at first deserted Aristotelianism for a physics based on atoms and the void, he found that there could be no real unity without an active principle. So he set out to restore the significance of substantial forms, understanding them more adequately than he had originally been able to do.

> *Je trouvai donc que leur nature consiste dans la force, et que de cela s'ensuit quelque chose d'analogique au sentiment et à l'appétit; et qu'ainsi il fallait les concevoir à l'imitation de la notion que nous avons des âmes. . . . Aristote les appelle entéléchies premières. Je les appelle, peut-être plus intelligiblement, forces primitives, qui ne contiennent pas seulement l'acte ou le complément de la possibilité, mais encore une activité originale.*[2]

Substance, for Leibniz, was essentially force; the notion of substance was not simply of something actual as

[1] *Op. cit.*, § 139.
[2] Leibniz: *Système Nouveau de la Nature*, § 3.

opposed to merely possible, but was an original conception of activity or agency itself.

A similar point of view can be found in the psychologically richer, although metaphysically less exact, exposition of Maine de Biran. Understanding by substance merely an ultimate substratum, he leaves the concept of substance aside, but he is, in reality, inquiring into the nature of substance when he investigates the awareness of the self. He finds the self in the consciousness of effort, not merely in the sensations and movements in which effort issues but in the originating effort which is the inner activity of the self. He might, perhaps, have cast his net wider, but he does succeed in enforcing the primitive character of the notion of agency and its relevance to the awareness of the self.

## § 3

Substance is, as everyone knows, an Aristotelian term, and it behoves us to ask how these theories of substance stand to the system of Aristotle himself. Certainly, when we look at the analysis of substance in the *Metaphysics*, the approach is mainly from the direction of logic, in harmony with the general character of the *Metaphysics*, of which the central portion is a kind of critique of pure reason or discussion of the application to fact of the categories of thought, although on a very different basis from the critique of Kant. There substance appears as the ultimate subject; substance in the primary sense, the individual existent, is that which can significantly be only the subject of a proposition. Yet we should not forget to bring the *Metaphysics* into relation with the *Physics*, and in the latter work we are reminded that every substance is a nature, a principle of change, activity and development. What, too, is the basis of the tentative identification of the formal, efficient and final causes?[1] It can only be that the formal element,

[1] Aristotle: *Physics* II, 198a.

what a thing is, is at the same time a tendency towards its natural end or fulfilment, and an active tendency bringing about that fulfilment in so far as circumstances permit. Consequently, if we take an adequate view of Aristotle's doctrine of substance, it is not lacking in dynamic character.

Nor was this character of substance overlooked by the Aristotelian scholastics. Aquinas, for example, is full of affirmations like the following: "A natural thing, by the form which establishes it in its kind, has a tendency towards its proper activities; for, as anything is, so it acts and tends towards those things appropriate to itself."[1] Hence the scholastics did not hesitate to speak of a natural appetite, *appetitus naturalis*, even in inanimate things, for they held that the dynamic factor in their being was closely analogous to desire and will. Perhaps, however, as scholasticism became less creative and more static itself, the dynamic element in the notion of substance came to be less stressed, and the static element became preponderant. This would explain how Descartes seems to have considered the latter exclusively, and how Leibniz thought he was making an innovation, and was in fact regarded as so doing, when he was only rediscovering an integral part of the genuine Aristotelian notion of substance.

In truth the idea of substance does not make sense without a dynamic element, for it is left without content. If substance were only the inert and featureless substratum which Locke makes it, it would be more reasonable to follow Hume's example and to dismiss it as a piece of philosophical mythology. Alternatively, one could follow Descartes and attribute the unity of the self to the continuous activity of thinking. But, if there is a distinctive notion of force which is logically prior to its manifestation in attributes and acts, so that these have to be regarded as the products of substantial force in given circumstances, the idea of substance acquires

[1] St. Thomas Aquinas: *Summa contra Gentiles*, iv, 19.

content and importance. This involves making a discrimination between agency and what is usually by modern philosophers described as causality, the sequence of events in accordance with universal laws. That this discrimination has not been made clear is probably one reason why the significance of substance is overlooked. A substance, as such, will not be a cause in the sense of a temporal antecedent, but it will essentially be an agent or force in relation to its acts and attributes. It remains to be seen whether this notion of substance can be justified by experience and reflection.

§ 4

A somewhat abstract but nevertheless helpful approach to the matter can be made by way of the analysis of an existential proposition. When we tell the sentimental humanitarian that men who like war for its own sake really exist, this statement is on a different logical plane from the statement that such men are a menace to civilization. In the latter case we are attributing the character of being a menace to civilization to an already recognized class of men, those who like war for its own sake, but in the former we are not in the same way presupposing this class of men and attributing existence to them, for, unless they existed, there would be no such class to which anything could be attributed. It is, perhaps, even more obvious that, when we say that Utopia does not exist, we are not denying the attribute of existence to a recognized thing called Utopia; we are rather saying that there is no such thing. In other words, as Aquinas and Kant both pointed out in their different ways in opposition to the ontological argument, existence is not a genuine attribute because it is presupposed to anything which can properly be called an attribute.

The meaning of a sentence of the form *X exists* should, then, be exhibited in such a manner as to show its difference from a sentence in which the grammatical predicate is a genuine act or attribute. In *The dog is black* and *The dog wags its tail*, the dog is the logical as well as the grammatical subject, but *The dog exists* means rather that something possesses the characteristics which make up the nature of the dog in question. Here the grammatical subject is logically the predicate, and the grammatical predicate of existence turns out to be the logical subject. So far this is plain sailing, but the ensuing remarks bring out consequences which are less commonly acknowledged.

Making a point which first received due emphasis from Aquinas, we may note that existence and individuality are one. Existence is not a universal like other universals. When I say that this is red and that is red, I mean that these two things are simply alike in being red. The redness is not really the same in both, for they are different things; it is an identity in difference, and the identity is inseparable from the difference except in thought, but the abstract redness, as far as it goes, is a factor of simple likeness. Existence, however, does not merely entail individual difference, but includes individuality in its very meaning; as the fundamental principle of individuality, it is primarily a factor of unlikeness in things, and only secondarily, in so far as there is a likeness in the mode of unlikeness, has that unity of meaning which makes it significant to say that this exists and that exists. This peculiarity of existence gives rise to the metaphysical theory of the analogy of being.

It would be out of place here to examine the metaphysical issues, but it is not irrelevant to suggest the bankruptcy of a philosophy which neglects the notion of the individual existent. Hume, for instance, formally denies the occurrence of universals as distinctive terms of thought, but in a deeper sense, by neglecting the individual subject and recognizing only impressions and ideas, he builds his whole world out of objects which are very like universals in so far as they do not seem to contain any factor incapable of description in universal terms. The same judgment can be passed on the more Humian of contemporary sense-data theorists; their worlds seem to contain no real things but only subsistent combinations of universals.

Returning to the main line of thought, we ask what is the relation between that ultimate subject to which individual existence primarily belongs and the attributes and acts in which it manifests itself. It may or may not manifest these particular attributes and acts. Even if there are attributes which necessarily result from it, it differs from them as the fundamental principle of individuality and being from factors which, considered in the abstract, are verifiable in other things or universal, but upon which it confers existence and individuality. Moreover, the relation of the subject to its attributes can be conceived only as the being such as to manifest these attributes or as the being such as in these circumstances to manifest these attributes and in other circumstances those others. The subject is a variable with its intrinsic law of variation. It is from this relationship of the subject to its attributes and acts that we derive the notion of an agent and a force. The ultimate subject, to which existence and individuality primarily belong, is characterized by the law of manifestation of the attributes and acts which receive existence and individuality from it. If we lose sight of this notion of the individual existent, the world becomes a shadowy interplay of universals, and the resultant philosophy bears upon it the mark of unreality.

These abstract considerations are, in fact, verified by experience. What is the self to which we refer our attributes and acts? It is precisely the ultimate subject of individual existence. It does not have to be sought in any one specific sort of experience, as Maine de Biran sought it in the experience of voluntary effort, but it is present in every sort of experience. When we are conscious that we are corporeal, we are not merely aware of the system of universals which is a mass of such volume and such density, but we are aware that we, as individual existents, possess such a mass and are such as, in the given circumstances, to possess it. When we are conscious that we have a sense-impression of red, the reality present to our minds is not merely a red visual expanse of such a shade and such dimensions, but it is our individual selves possessing this impression. When we are conscious that we are thinking, we are truly conscious that *we* are thinking and not merely conscious of a thought.

That is why our experiences give us pleasure or pain. Sensations do not feel pleasure or pain; it is we who feel pleasure or pain because this sensation is a fulfilment of our nature and that other is a frustration. A realization of the tension between the essential self and its actual experience is necessary in order to make feeling and emotion intelligible. Still more clearly are we conscious of ourselves as substances and agents, and here we do justice to Maine de Biran, in the experience of volition, of consciously directing our being towards the performance of such and such acts and the possession of such and such qualities. It is strange that the notion of substance should have so often been neglected in modern times, when it is so intimately present to us in every moment of experience. The grounds of this neglect can be found only in the impoverishment of the notion of substance which reduces it to an inert substratum, and in an exclusive preoccupation with knowing to the disadvantage of feeling and willing, where the ultimate self can scarcely be overlooked. Even so, it is not a readily comprehensible oversight.

We are conscious, then, not only of sensations, and of the body in so far as it transmits the stimulus of sensation, but also of ourselves as thinking, feeling and willing, and as distinct from the specific acts of thought, feeling and will. We are conscious of the self in relation to its attributes and acts. There is no bare consciousness of the essential self, but, when we are conscious of attributes and acts, we are at the same time conscious of the self as possessing them. As Aquinas puts it, the mind is aware of itself, not in its essence apart, but through its acts; yet this is not a process of inference from its acts, for in its acts it becomes simply present to itself.[1]

The ultimate individual existent self is the subject of attributes and acts, mental and corporeal. It is such as, in these circumstances, to manifest such activities and, in other circumstances, to manifest others. It is not an agent of unlimited power, for external circumstances are the conditions which largely govern its actual manifestations. But it is a genuine agent, a force, tending towards some modes of being and away from others, feeling some experiences as fulfilments and others as frustrations. We are, in relation to our specific experiences, conscious of ourselves as substances and agents.

[1] Cf. St. Thomas Aquinas: *Summa Theologica* I, qu. 87, art. iii c.

## CHAPTER VI

# THE EXTERNAL WORLD

## § 1

When the question is asked how we come to know the external world, this presumably means the world external to our bodies. To speak of a world external to our minds would be to use a highly ambiguous and misleading phrase. Everything that we genuinely know except our mental activities themselves are external to the mind in the sense that the object of awareness is presupposed to the awareness of it; in another sense everything that we know is inside the mind because we know it. Inside and outside, however, can only be applied to the mind metaphorically, and on a serious philosophical issue metaphors are best avoided.

In reality the question about the external world concerns not only spatial objects, to which externality is literally applicable, but also other minds. Hence it can be put in a more general form by asking how we come to know things other than ourselves. This is more adequate, provided that we remember that there are undoubtedly facts about our present selves of which we can have no direct consciousness and which, consequently, if they are to be known at all, must be known in the same manner as things other than ourselves. The direct consciousness of the body does not extend to the whole organism; hence there are parts of the body which we can know only as we know external objects. Certainly when one hand touches the other, there is not only a consciousness of each hand but a perceptual awareness of each in relation to the other which does not differ in principle, whatever that principle may turn out to be, from the perceptual awareness of any other material object with which we come into contact. Modern psychology, too, makes considerable capital out of facts about the mind which do not enter into consciousness, and some of its suggestions are no doubt justified. Therefore, while we are primarily investigating how we come to be aware of trees and rocks, chairs and tables, animals and other men, our investigation should not be conceived so narrowly as to exclude facts about ourselves of which direct consciousness is unavailable.

Berkeley, of course, while admitting a knowledge of other minds, will tell us not only that we cannot be aware of material things independent of mind but that, if we reflect for a moment, we shall not even suppose ourselves to be aware of them. Material things are simply systems of sense-qualities; an orange is the combination of its visual shape and colour, its tactile shape and feel, its taste and its smell. When we have once recognized that these sense-qualities are no more than contents of consciousness, we are bound to admit that the orange exists only in the consciousness of some mind. It is true that oranges, and still more the dishes upon which they are placed, have a curious permanence, or perhaps it would be better to say recurrence to mind, by which they appear to be independent of our consciousness, but this can be explained, without invoking the hypothesis of material substance, by their being objects of the divine mind.

It is not to be denied that the Berkeleyan simplification of the universe has the attraction which belongs to all simplifications, and it would dispense us from any further inquiry except into the knowledge of other minds. Nevertheless the truth cannot be hidden that we do in fact mean by a material thing more than Berkeley would have us mean. We mean a substance, or a collection of substances, with a certain volume and density, in a certain spatial relation to our bodies, stimulating the sensations which help us to discern its nature. In the pragmatic thinking of ordinary life we scarcely discriminate the sensations which are signs of the object from the object itself; philosophical reflection enables us to make this discrimination, but it does not abolish the external object. We still know what we mean by a material thing independent of mind, and we still believe that such things exist. Whether this belief be valid or mistaken, whether we be capable of reaching certainty on the question or not, it still presents itself as an obligatory field of inquiry.

If we do turn out to have knowledge of material things other than our bodies, this will be a different sort of knowledge from consciousness. In consciousness the object of knowledge is physically present to and united with the awareness of it; perceptual knowledge will be of things distinct and even distant from the percipient. Therefore, as we have already noticed when dealing with sensation, it would be futile to proceed like some of our sense-data theorists and to attempt to construct the material world out of the contents of consciousness. Any construction out of sense-data will have the same subjectivity as the sense-data themselves; it may be a Berkeleyan material thing, but it is not what we spontaneously suppose a material thing to be. Sense-data are a reflection of the material world, but they are not the material world.

By thinkers who have realized the wide difference between the kind of knowledge which is consciousness and the kind of knowledge which is an awareness of things other than ourselves, it has often been tacitly assumed that perceptual experience must really be the result of inference. There is no general ground in the nature of knowledge why there should not be a direct awareness of things other than the self; any alleged principle of this sort would depend on the erroneous supposition that awareness is in some spatial sense inside the subject. Nevertheless the question of fact remains to be examined. We have to see whether in fact it is exclusively by inference or not that we come to know things other than the self.

In examining inferential theories of perception we have to consider not only whether the suggested type of inference is valid but also whether it is really the way in which perceptual experience naturally develops. It might be that there was a valid process of inference by which we could make the transition from consciousness to the external world, but that at the same time this was unnecessary and alien from our natural mental processes. Hence the validity of an inferential theory would not disprove the existence of direct knowledge of the external world; that question would still have to be considered on its own account as well.

## § 2

The first modern theory of perception is an inferential one. Descartes, of course, does not begin from the data of consciousness as we have described them. He does not admit a direct awareness of the body; what we are conscious of consists simply of the thinking self and its ideas. The problem which faces him is that of the validity of our ideas of the material world, including our own bodies.[1]

That these ideas are not the product of his own will is obvious; they cannot, therefore, be causally attributed to him as a thinking being in the rather narrow sense of explicit thought and will in which Descartes conceives the thinking self. Their cause may be either bodies which they represent or some superior power, God or another spirit. How is the decision to be made between these alternatives?

The first point which Descartes makes is that already, prior to rational reflection, he spontaneously believes that bodies exist corresponding with his ideas of them.

---

[1] Cf. Descartes: *Metaphysical Meditations* VI. The most balanced interpretation is that of A. K. Stout: "Descartes' Proof of the Existence of Matter," in *Mind*, April, 1932, pp. 191–207.

Reflection teaches him that not all his spontaneous beliefs are accurate; he can no longer, when he has thought a little, attribute the secondary qualities of colour, sound and the rest to external things, nor can he rely on his first vague estimates of shape and size. But certain elements remain which are clear and distinct, and are not susceptible of being corrected by reflection; it still appears that there are bodies extended in three dimensions, that among these is one closely connected with his own mind, that his sensations give him information about this body which is his own, and that there are surrounding bodies some of which are useful to him and others harmful. These beliefs, which are incorrigible by reflection, are the teaching of nature in the full sense of the phrase.

It is still, however, possible to doubt whether the teaching of nature is true. But, when he reflects that the author of his nature is a good God who cannot will to deceive, it appears that there is a contradiction between the veracity of God and the hypothesis that he is bound by nature to entertain false beliefs which he has no means of correcting. From the veracity of God, therefore, follows a rational certainty that the teaching of nature is true. He has no longer only an incorrigible but non-rational belief in the existence of the material world; he knows that bodies exist.

This argument is not without force. It seems to be true that a benevolent Creator could not provide us with a nature impelling us towards a false belief which we had no means of correcting. Psychologically, perhaps, it is not a very useful line of thought, since there appear to be comparatively few people, at any rate nowadays, who are more certain of the existence of their Creator than they are of that of the material world. Logically, however, the existence of the material world can hardly be said to be presupposed to a demonstration of the existence of God, so that Descartes' argument cannot be dismissed on that account. Nevertheless it still remains questionable whether such an argument is necessary; there may be a more natural and direct route to the external world.

This point is reinforced when we consider the status of the kind of belief which Descartes describes as the teaching of nature. The name of reason, for this philosopher, is reserved to the reflective operations of mind according to explicit logical principles. With reason understood in this way is sharply contrasted the teaching of nature as a blind and instinctive belief. Can this antithesis be upheld?

When we recall what our spontaneous thinking really is, it does not seem that it is so completely non-rational as Descartes would make it out to be. Certainly it is very different from a reflective process of thought in which we bring before our minds what are the premisses and what is the conclusion, and estimate precisely what degree of probability the evidence confers upon the conclusion to which we incline. Nevertheless spontaneous thinking is not blind credulity. When you tell me that you breakfasted to-day, I probably accept the statement without further demur and without explicitly weighing the likelihood of your having done anything so customary or the unlikelihood of your wishing to deceive me about anything so trivial. But, if you tell me that the end of the world is occurring to-morrow, my spontaneous reaction is already other than unquestioning acceptance; I want to know what evidence you have for so startling an affirmation.

In other words, however rapid and unreflective my spontaneous thinking may be, it is not entirely different from an exact and scientific weighing of evidence. The two kinds of thought differ rather as the implicit from the explicit, the confused from the distinct, the unreflective from the reflective. The human mind, even at its most irrational, still retains traces of rationality; for any belief, however wild, there is always a reason, however poor and however inadequate. That is why mere dismissal is never sound criticism; genuine criticism, even of what would commonly be regarded as absurd, is an endeavour to find the reason for the assertion, to make clear its inadequacy and to show in what direction it should properly lead.

If this is true even of wild theories, it is doubly true of common beliefs. A natural unreflective process of thought still deserves to be treated as a process of thought. If people spontaneously believe that there is a material world, as they do, the philosopher cannot treat this as a blind assumption irrelevant to his reflections. He should rather ask why they have this belief. It might conceivably turn out that their grounds were inadequate, and that the facts really suggested something rather different, but it is, in any case, his duty to examine these grounds. Descartes, by treating spontaneous beliefs as completely non-rational, condemned himself to follow a curiously circuitous path to the material world. By making explicit and reflecting upon the implicit and unreflective process of thought by which belief in the material world is attained, it may be that he could have discovered a more direct route to his objective.

§ 3

Locke is the typical example of a philosopher who sought to interpret on an inferential basis the natural process by which we come to a knowledge of the external world.[1] His arguments are reducible to a consideration of our passivity in respect of sensations and the systematic consistency of sensations themselves. That sensations depend upon the appropriate sense-organs is evident because a man deprived of a sense-organ can never have the corresponding kind of sensation. But sensations are not produced simply by the sense-organs themselves; "for then the eyes of a man in the dark would produce

[1] Cf. Locke: *Essay on the Human Understanding*, Bk. IV, ch. xi.

colours, and his nose smell roses in the winter: but we see nobody gets the relish of a pineapple till he goes to the Indies where it is, and tastes it".

Images are, partly at any rate, dependent upon the will, but we find not only that we cannot have sensations at will but that, when we do have them, we cannot avoid having them as long as the sense-organ is open to stimulation. While images generally leave the emotions unaffected, sensations give us a definite pleasure or pain which can easily be seen to be due to the recognition of a real object and no mere appearance. Moreover, the different senses support one another; when we really see, and do not imagine, a fire, we have the sensation of heat as well.

The weakness of the details of this argument scarcely needs comment, for the weakness of the argument as a whole is so obvious. Locke has, in fact, given no reason at all why the consistency of sensations and our passivity in their regard should lead us to suppose that they are due to the action of material things upon us. Nothing that he says is incompatible with the cause of sensations being some superior spirit or malignant demon such as Descartes summoned up before his mind as a preliminary hypothesis. Nothing that he says is incapable of being explained on Berkeleyan principles by which sensations acquire their systematic and compelling character from a cosmic mind to which all ideas first belong.

Locke himself is aware that his demonstration is not all that it might be. He tries to pass it off with a few jaunty remarks about the man who likes to suppose that he is dreaming and is therefore only dreaming the objection to which he wants a waking man to reply. Apart from this bluff, however, he confesses that, if anyone still wishes to doubt the existence of the external world, he has no absolutely peremptory argument by which to convince him. Nevertheless he maintains that the argument is as strong as the human mind has the right to expect, and can be justified on pragmatic grounds as leading to suitable behaviour for attaining pleasure and avoiding pain.

Locke, then, holds that the causal argument from sensations to the material world is of such high probability as to amount to practical certainty. One is inclined to ask, by the way, why, if the process by which we come to a belief in the material world is an argument from effect to cause, we conclude to the specific part of the cause which we in fact select. When we hear a noise and say that a train is passing, the train is only one among a set of conditions at a particular stage of the causal process which finally results in our hearing the noise. If we are really arguing from effect to cause, why do we not conclude equally to the rest of the causal conditions?

The fundamental difficulty, however, is that the causal argument cannot truly be said to yield a high probability for the existence of the material world. If we take our sensations as the sole basis of argument, their independence of our desires, their consistency among themselves and our passivity in their regard certainly lead us to look for causes outside ourselves. A world of material things is, no doubt, one of the possible types of cause which we might assign to sensations. But it is only one possible type of cause; other hypotheses might be supposed, and the real cause might be something entirely different from anything that we are able to imagine. Sensations presumably have causes other than ourselves, but, unless we have some stronger reason for believing in the existence of a material world, it would be more prudent to confess that the nature of their causes was unknown. On the causal argument alone, the material world remains an unrefuted but quite unproved hypothesis.

A causal argument should, consequently, be admitted to yield only a low probability for the existence of the material world. There can be no doubt, of course, that

common-sense thinking frequently confuses high probability with certainty; practical certainty means a probability so high that the alternative can for practical purposes be neglected. In matters remote from his customary
sphere of thought and conduct the ordinary man sometimes confuses low probability with certainty; his judgments, shall we say, of the merits of foreign forms of
government are, upon occasion, as vehement in expression
as they are deficient in reason. But the man who, in
matters which belong to his customary sphere of thought
and conduct, confuses low probability with certainty is
precisely the lunatic. If, then, the universal human
conviction that a material world exists is an attribution
of certainty to a probability of so low an order as is
yielded by the causal argument, it would seem that we
are a race of madmen. It really appears inconceivable
that, on a question so fundamental and of such universal
relevance as the existence of the material world, we
should all have arrived spontaneously at an untroubled
certainty on so weak a basis as is afforded by the causal
argument. Much, doubtless, of our knowledge of the
external world is inferential, but it can scarcely all be
inferential. The weakness which the causal argument
reveals to reflection is a sign that we should look once
again to see whether there is not some more direct
acquaintance with the external world.

## § 4

It cannot be denied that the supposition of a direct
acquaintance with some external objects runs counter
to the prevailing tendencies of modern philosophy. If
we seek support among the historic names, we shall
find it almost exclusively in that group of Scottish
philosophers of whom the chief were Reid and Hamilton.
Reid asserts energetically, as the deliverance of his
reflection, that upon the occasion of sensation we have

at the same time a direct perception of the external world, but he makes no attempt to explain how this is possible. He declares, indeed, that the conjunction of sensation and perception is mysterious, and has to be accepted as brute fact. Hamilton provides a more exact analysis and refutation of the grounds on which intuitive perception is denied, and confines such direct acquaintance to objects in immediate contact with the sense-organ. Even Hamilton, however, does not set out to analyse the conditions of intuition and to show positively how direct perception is possible. Conviction can hardly become complete until such an attempt has been made.

Meanwhile there is still a certain amount of work to be done in clearing the ground. We have already noticed that there can be no general principle excluding direct acquaintance with things other than the subject. The cognitive act belongs to the subject, and in that sense it is in the subject, but it is not a spatial thing, and there is no reason, on that account, why its reference should be confined to the subject. In fact, on a general view, knowing is precisely the means by which the limits of a subject's being are transcended.

There is, however, a more specific reason why perception has been assumed to be inferential. Perception undoubtedly occurs in connection with consciousness or awareness of the present self; it is when we have consciousness that we think ourselves to perceive external things, and, when we have no appropriate state of consciousness, we certainly have no perception of the external world. How, then, is consciousness related to perception? It might seem that the state of consciousness is the whole cause of the perception. But to say that one cognitive act is the whole cause of another cognitive act is only another way of saying that their contents are related as logical antecedent and consequent. If the consciousness is really the whole cause of the perception, we cannot avoid admitting that there is an inference from consciousness to perception.

94

The alternatives must be made clear in order that we may see what we have to assert if we are going to uphold the intuitive character of perception. If, whenever we have a certain state of consciousness, we have also a certain perception, there is at least an implicit inference from consciousness to perception. If there cannot be that state of consciousness unless there exists a material thing of the sort of which we claim to have the corresponding perception, this inference is valid. Otherwise the degree of probability to be assigned to the inference varies directly with the degree of probability with which the occurrence of the state of consciousness indicates the existence of the material thing. But we have already seen that, arguing from consciousness alone, it is impossible to attribute any high degree of probability to the existence of the material world. Hence the degree of probability to be assigned in this case to the inference from consciousness to perception is itself small. If, therefore, whenever we have a certain state of consciousness, we believe ourselves also to have a certain perception, we must admit not only that there is an inference from consciousness to perception, but also that this is an extremely dubious inference.

We can escape this consequence only if we deny that specific perceptions invariably follow specific states of consciousness. An intuitive theory of perception is perfectly compatible with the generalization that, whenever there is perception, there is consciousness; it is incompatible with the generalization that, whenever there is a certain state of consciousness, there is a certain perception. On an intuitive account the cause of perception must be held to be not the consciousness alone but the consciousness together with the real external object perceived. The truth that we do not have perception without consciousness has led many thinkers to reverse the relation and to suppose that perception is the invariable sequel of the appropriate consciousness. That this does not follow is elementary logic, for it is the fallacy of affirming the consequent, but we must see on its own account that it is not true if we are with complete confidence to uphold an intuitive theory of perception.

At the present stage of the history of philosophy this is evidently a highly contentious question. That is why it is useful to approach it circuitously by first investigating the conditions of memory. Memory is parallel to perception, in so far as it extends our awareness in the dimension of time while perception extends our awareness in the field of space. If we can discover what kind of knowledge memory is and what are its conditions, it is likely to throw light on the more controversial question of perception.

## CHAPTER VII

# MEMORY

§ 1

THERE is a wealth of psychological literature on the subject of memory, but philosophers have treated it in an oddly perfunctory manner. We are told of the mental apparatus and conditions of memory, we hear of its normal functioning and of its aberrations, but the essential epistemological or philosophical question usually remains unanswered. This is the question of the logical status of the belief that we have a knowledge of the past.

For it is memory in this fullest sense which is of primary interest to the philosopher. Memory is, of course, often employed in other senses. When present behaviour is conditioned by the past, even though there is no revival of any image of the past, this may be said to be an instance of memory. The burnt child dreads the fire, even though he does not explicitly recall the original burning. The contemporary psychopathologist finds that many mental disorders can be relieved by raising these latent memories to the stage of explicit recall.

There is memory in a fuller sense when there is the reproduction of an image resembling some past experience. All imagery partakes of the nature of memory in this sense, in so far as every element in it is derived from past experience, although the free imagination may build up elements derived from the past in such new combinations that their derivation is far from obvious. The more purely reproductive the imagery is, the more it has of the nature of memory. The spontaneous revival of images of things which we have seen or heard or sensed in some other way is a sufficiently familiar occurrence, and it is curious to note how greatly the power of visual or of auditory reproduction varies with different minds. The laws of association of ideas bring to light the principles upon which images revive, the ways in which any experience summons up the images of experiences related to it whether by their intrinsic nature or by their previous occurrence in conjunction. First formulated by Aristotle in the *De Memoria et Reminiscentia,* the laws of association have been fully explored by later psychologists.

All this is psychology, but the philosopher finds a problem of greater moment for his purposes in memory in the fullest sense, in recollection or reminiscence. When we do not merely in fact reproduce an image of the past, but explicitly judge that we had an experience of a similar kind in the past, the nature of this cognitive act demands investigation. It evidently does not take place unless we have in the present an image or revival of the past experience which we claim to recollect. There must also be in our minds a notion of past time, and it is not difficult to see that the awareness of the brief stretch of time which is the real present of consciousness allows an ideal extension either into the past or into the future. It might be supposed that recollection was simply the association of a present image with some more or less clearly defined position in past time. Indeed this is probably the tacit assumption of many thinkers, for otherwise they would have shown greater realization that the analysis of memory is of considerable epistemological interest.

That this explanation is very far from adequate becomes clear on reflection. It should be observed that there is properly no such thing as an image of past time; an image is necessarily something present. To conceive of past time can only be an intellectual act; apart from the awareness of some real event in the past, the bare notion of past time is a conceptual supposal. Hence recollection is not simply a fusion of images; it is at least the association of an image with a concept.

But this is still not enough. For we do not attribute the

image itself to the past. The image is plainly present, but we claim to be aware of something like it belonging to the past. This is not another image, for it is past; it can only be the object of an intellectual act. Hence the linking of the present image and the awareness of it as present with the conception of past time is not an explanation of memory; on the contrary, this can only be explained through memory. The image and the awareness of it belong of themselves to the present, and do not bear upon themselves the mark of the past. If we link them with the past, it must be because we are aware, or think ourselves to be aware, of an experience in the past resembling the present image. The act of memory still remains to be explained.

Is the act of memory an inference of some kind? That memory is often inferential is evident for the simple reason that memory is fallible. If all memory were a direct awareness of the past, it would be infallible. Yet people often think that they remember something and turn out to be mistaken. It is unnecessary to labour the point; we have all come across instances of this, both in ourselves and in others. George IV may have believed, in the end, that he really remembered being present at the battle of Waterloo.

If some ostensible instances of memory are cases of mistaken inference, it is probable that some genuine memories are the result of valid inference. But it is wholly incredible that all instances of memory should be inferential. Consider ourselves with only the data of consciousness at our disposal. We have as yet no reason to believe that anything has existed at any time other than the present of which we are conscious. We may suppose that we have solved the problem of perception and can discern what elements of present experience are due to external stimulation. There remain a number of factors of a similar kind, which we find that we cannot attribute causally to the external world. We may well wonder how they arise, but there seems to be no reason whatever why we should jump to the conclusion that they are the result of past experiences, and in some cases approximate reproductions of past experiences. This would, no doubt, be a possible hypothesis, but there would be no means of testing it, and it is not easy to see why it should occur to us at all. Surely, if we were left to draw conclusions from the data of consciousness alone, the causes of what we now call images would be for ever unknown, and we should remain ignorant even that we had existed at any moment before the present.

Hence it is necessary to admit some cases of direct or intuitive knowledge of the past in order to explain not only why we place reliance on memory but even why we believe ourselves to have memory at all. Given that in some instances we have intuitive memory, and that from these we begin to understand how the past tends to reproduce itself in experience, it is possible to see how, in other cases, where intuitive memory is absent, we take it upon ourselves to infer our past from our present. Such inferences have greater or less probability; they lead sometimes to truth and sometimes to error. Nevertheless the very fact that we are inclined to make them testifies to the occurrence of cases of intuitive memory in which inference is unnecessary.

Reid had the good sense to admit the existence of intuitive memory.[1] Hamilton, in his notes, contradicts him, saying that "an *immediate* knowledge of a *past* thing is a contradiction. For we can only know a thing immediately, if we know it in itself, or as existing; but what is past cannot be known in itself, for it is non-existent".[2] Here Hamilton, who accurately exposes the fallacy of thinking that the scope of immediate knowledge must be spatially limited to the subject of knowledge, falls, apparently without any misgiving, straight into the parallel error of supposing that the

---

[1] Reid: *Essays on the Intellectual Powers*, essay III.
[2] Hamilton's *Reid*, p. 339n.

scope of immediate knowledge must be temporally limited to the present in which the act of knowing occurs. There is no more reason for the one assertion than for the other. Just as knowing, by its nature, is a means of transcending the limitations of the subject in space, so it is a means of transcending the limitations of the subject in time. Reid is correct in maintaining that there are instances of intuitive memory. But he does not analyse the conditions under which intuitive memory occurs; in fact he professes his inability to do so. An attempt must be made to supply the lack.

§ 2

Consider the case in which the memory of a particular event in the past occurs clearly and spontaneously. I see a book on someone's table and read the title; then I remember that So-and-so said to me the other day that I ought not to miss it. I may have a visual image of the speaker; I certainly have an auditory image of the words he used. My memory is not the awareness of these images, for they are contents of consciousness in the present, but it is evident that I could not remember the past unless I had these present images. Although my memory of the past event is thus psychologically dependent upon the presence of images, it is plainly not a simple logical consequence of them. I am not inferring from the images to the past event; the memory occurs as spontaneously and immediately as the consciousness of the present images. Nor, if I were asked to justify my belief about the past, could I adequately do so by referring exclusively to these images; they do not afford a sufficient basis for such an inference. All that I can say is that I do clearly and unmistakably remember.

I find, therefore, that the facts of experience would be unintelligible unless I claimed in such cases an intuitive knowledge of the past. What are the conditions of this kind of intuition? One condition we have already noticed; this is the presence in consciousness of factors resembling the past event. I can recollect the past only to the extent that I can in this sense revive it in the present. What else is required in order that, in conjunction with the consciousness of these reproductive images, I should have an intuitive recollection? The general answer is not far to seek: it is when the past event is in the causal ancestry of my present similar consciousness. We have chosen for consideration the most favourable case; a clear image has come spontaneously to mind, resembling one, and only one, event in my recent past. So-and-so said to me that I ought not to miss the book in question. A differential factor in the causal series determining the occurrence of this image was the actual past event; it must be because the image thus obtrudes itself upon my consciousness that I am able, not to infer from effect to cause, but to have an intuitive awareness of the past event which is a differential condition resembling it.

I know the event as a part of my past. I do not first form a concept of past time by extending backwards the brief stretch of time which is the present of consciousness, and then populate it with images. I do not in the proper sense populate it with images at all, for the images themselves are unmistakably present. Rather, given the present consciousness and the images which belong to it, I am at the same time and with equal logical immediacy stimulated to become aware of a past containing events resembling these images.

The sense of the length of time between the remembered event and the present introduces something more complex, for it postulates at least a vague memory of other events intervening. The exact dating of a past event is more complex still, for it is possible only through the use of symbols, linguistic and numerical. When I remember that something happened on the tenth of September of this year, I have a visual or auditory image of the words expressing this date and am judging from their association with the memory of some event that the event happened on that day. Here we must guard against the possible but futile suggestion that recollection consists simply in the association of images with dates, for dates, which are present symbols in consciousness, would have no meaning for us unless we already had some knowledge of the past. None of the more complex phenomena of memory are explicable unless there is some fundamental intuition of the past, due to a reproduction of the past in the present, causally attributable to the past event.

Consider now the vaguer case of recollection which is not the recollection of any one specific event in the past. When I remember that William the Conqueror came to the throne in 1066, I do not remember any specific instance in which I read or was told of this. If, instead of regarding it as a recollection, I did not know that it was not a free image formed by present fancy, I should not place any reliance upon it as an elementary piece of historical knowledge. Here I have a present image which I recognize at once to be a reproduction of my past experience, but which, since I have heard or read of the fact so many times, does not make me aware of any one event in my past. There is no one past event which is an exclusive differential condition of my having this image now; hence, while I am aware of the past through it, this awareness is confusedly of the past in general.

Consider, too, what happens when I am trying to remember something. This is really a case in which I already have some memory and am trying to remember more. At what times do the Guildford trains leave my local station? I remember that there are trains to Guildford; what fails to come is the time at which they leave. I try over the sound of various times in order to judge which is more readily associated with the train; I try, perhaps, to imagine the relevant page of the time-table or the voice of someone who once gave me the required information. Possibly there comes a flash of intuitive memory, more especially if I divert my attention for a moment in order to lessen the causal interference of my present anxiety to know, and to give play to the causality deriving from the past. Maybe the influence of the past is not strong enough, and I have no such flash of intuition; in the end I make a probable judgment in favour of one time or another on account of greater readiness of association, or I have to admit that I cannot make up my mind.

When there is no intuitive memory, we have, then, to fall back upon a process of inference based on the ease of association of images in the present. Such an inference must usually be less than certain, and inferences of this kind are evidently the source of those errors of memory which are so frequent. Since all imagery has a foundation in past experience, it tends to retain a certain flavour of the past, and it is not difficult to make a hasty inference that we are remembering when we are merely imagining. But, once again, it is very clear that we could not begin to make such inferences simply from our present experience, without having some more direct knowledge of the past and some conception based on this of how memory works. The typical instance of memory, from which the other phenomena of memory acquire intelligibility, remains the intuition of a past experience which is a differential condition of a present image unambiguously resembling it.

§ 3

It should be noticed that all awareness of change is dependent upon memory. We do not strictly see a thing move. Where there is change, there is a succession of nows which cannot be embraced in one real present. The impression that we see things moving is due to the rather complex relation between sensation and perception, which has still to be discussed. We can, however, anticipate by pointing out that sensations overlap, and that we often have at the same time present to consciousness a number of sensations which we perceptually interpret as indicating successive stages in a process of change outside us. The awareness, however, of the order in which these sensations appeared supposes memory.

Even without going beyond consciousness to perceptual objects, the hearing of a melody, for example, is more complex than we might at first suppose it to be. It is not to hear the notes one by one without relation to one another, nor is it to hear them as one jumble of sound. You hear a melodic phrase when all its notes are at the same time present to consciousness but you are aware of their successive inception and of their consequent temporal relations one with another. This would not be possible without memory. The inception of each new note is a change which introduces a new real present; without memory this present would be shut off from the past. It is sufficiently evident, too, that in such cases we do not have to attain a problematic past by an elaborate process of inference. In the example chosen the past is not even reviving itself in the present; it is actually continuing itself into the present, and through its compelling influence on the present we are immediately aware of it as the proximate past. The ease with which we recognize change is another sign of the existence of intuitive memory.

This type of experience enables us to assign an exact meaning to the specious present as opposed to the real present. It is not asserted to be the meaning actually intended in psychological discussion, for it is sometimes hard to say what this is. It would, however, be a workable definition of the specious present to say that it included that part of the past which is continued without interruption into the present and which is consequently first among the objects of intuitive memory.

Finally, the recognition of intuitive memory, together with the validity of the notion of substance, removes the puzzle which has sometimes been thought to attach to the question of personal identity. In the absence of an adequate notion of substance Locke involves himself in labyrinthine difficulties on the matter.[1] Memory, instead of being a consequence of identity, becomes its source, so that you can apparently have no real identity except in so far as you can remember. In reality memory is not simply of events in the past but of events in my past; I am immediately aware of myself, the same substance and agent as now, having had certain experiences in the past. With this direct knowledge of a continuing self as the subject of successive experiences, there is no difficulty in conceiving that self as having existed at times of which no memory now comes to mind.

Nor is there any difficulty in conceiving the continuance of the same self even if memory completely fails. The empirical facts of mental dissociation yield an appearance of multiple personality; they do not compel us to accept its reality. To overcome the dissociation and to reunite the strands of memory and habit is obviously the proper aim of treatment, and its feasibility in many cases is a sign that multiple personality is not more than apparent. Identical personality must be conceived in a metaphysical way as a continuing substance or agent, whose continuance is normally revealed by memory, but whose identity is the source of the possibility of memory and not its result. Having glanced at these corollaries of memory, we return to the question of the perception of the external world with a view of applying to it what we have learned from the cognate question of memory.

[1] Locke: *Essay on the Human Understanding*, Bk. II, ch. xxvii.

## CHAPTER VIII

# THE CONDITIONS OF PERCEPTION

§ 1

WE have seen reason to believe that there must be some intuitive knowledge of the external world, although we have not yet discovered when and how this comes to be. Turning to memory, we saw that there must be intuitive knowledge of our own past, and we assigned as its condition the occurrence of a present content of consciousness through the causality of a past experience which it unambiguously resembles. In a word, intuitive memory is due to the assimilation of the present to the past under the influence of the past, or to a communication between the past and the present. Is there an analogous assimilation, or communication between the external world and ourselves, which would make intuitive perception intelligible?

When I reflect on sensation in the strict meaning of the word, on the proper sensibles or secondary qualities, I find no basis for any such intuition. When I hear a whistle, I have no immediate awareness of anything outside me possessing the quality of sound of which I am conscious. In fact I find no reason to believe that any purely material thing does possess such a quality; it seems to be a typical event in the history of a sentient subject. Similarly, I am not tempted to believe that the orange itself possesses the qualities of taste and smell of which I am conscious. Colours, too, although they are very closely associated with external things in my common-sense thinking, do not appear, upon reflection, to be qualities of them; they also belong exclusively to me as a sentient subject.

In conjunction with sensation, however, we found

that there was a consciousness of the part of the bodily organism which transmitted the stimulus of sensation. We are conscious of parts of the body as a mass, or volume with density, in a state of mechanical tension. Since the primary notion of body is that of mass, it seems likely that the clue to the perception of other bodies will be found in this consciousness. And surely it does provide the answer to our question. For it is in the experience of contact and mutual pressure that we find an intuition of other bodies for which sensation by itself affords no foundation.

When I press my hand against the arm of my chair, I am conscious of a certain tactile sense-quality which belongs to me as a sentient subject. I am also conscious of part of my hand as a mass which is being compressed. And at the same time I am aware of another mass, which is in fact the arm of the chair, with which I am in active contact. These three factors in experience are distinct. I might possess the tactile sense-quality without the consciousness of mass, as when I merely imagine my hand pressing against the chair. I might possess the consciousness of my hand being compressed without any awareness of an external object with which I am in contact; although the former is evidently a condition of the latter, it is not by itself a sufficient condition. I am not inferring from the one to the other, and it would be a highly problematic inference if I tried to do so. There might be all sorts of unknown causes other than external bodies which could produce in my hand the effect of compression. But in fact I am unmistakably aware of another body with which my hand is in contact, and this awareness can only be an instance of intuitive knowledge.

Here, on analysis, we find a situation parallel to that of intuitive memory. Among the conditions which determine me to a consciousness of my body is another body in mechanical interaction with it. There is communication of a physical quality of motion. Motion in the purely mathematical sense is not, of course, intended, for this is simply a change of external relationship between volumes. Motion in an intrinsic and physical sense is a a change of density, compression or expansion; a condition of density, the tension with which the body is held together, is a potential quality of motion. On active contact there is communication of such a quality of motion, and I have an intuitive perception of another body pressing against me.

While external contact thus provides a striking example of what we are seeking, we can at the same time see that the contact of one part of the body with another is the occasion of a similar intuition. Then there is a double consciousness and a double perception. I am conscious of the one part of the body and intuitively perceive the other in relation to it; I am conscious of the other part and perceive the one in relation to it. This is verified both in the incidental contact of, say, one hand with the other and in the internal mechanical interaction of adjacent parts of the organism. Indeed, since mechanical change is necessarily due to external causes, the consciousness of any part of the body is always accompanied by the intuition of a corporeal mass external to it, whether this be another part of the body or a completely external thing.

Moreover, since all sensation is preceded by a mechanical stimulus, and the consciousness of sensation redounds upon this, all sense-consciousness, as opposed to imagination, is accompanied by the perceptual intuition of a body external to the sense-organ. That is why we are able so readily to refer the data of sight, hearing, taste and smell to the action of external bodies. Nevertheless the perceptual intuition which occurs in connection with these senses is only of material things in contact with the sense-organ. Hence our customary employment of these senses for the discrimination of relatively distant objects is an instance not of intuitive perception but of perceptual inference.

As I look round the room, I am fully persuaded that it contains a desk, chairs and bookcases, but their existence can only be an inference from my visual data. If I had nothing but such data from which to infer, the belief that they were caused by external bodies would be an unrefuted but quite gratuitous hypothesis. It is because I have a genuinely intuitive perception of the chair in which I am sitting, and because I have at various times been in contact with the familiar objects in the room, that I am able so unhesitatingly to rely upon my sensations as indications of real bodies surrounding me. Since the intuitive basis of what we normally call perceptual experience is comparatively small, it is not so extraordinary that many philosophers have overlooked it. Yet, small though it may be, it is the indispensable condition of the practical reliability of perceptual inference. If we had no intuitive perception, we should not know that there was a material world outside us at all, and certainly could not build up the complex associations of different sorts of sensations with different sorts of bodies which serve us in our practical dealings with the world about us.

In general, then, the condition of the intuition of things other than our present selves is assimilation or communication. Whether in memory of the past or in perception of the external world, we have an intuitive awareness when there is present in consciousness a concrete factor specifically reproducing the object of intuition and due to its causality. That this should be so is not unintelligible. The way in which one thing may in a certain sense be present in another is by causal determination. Awareness, being of its nature capable of transcending the subject, finds the possibility of intuition in the causal presence of other things. There can, however, be no intuition where the causal conditions are unlike their effect. But there where is not only causation but the communication of a similar quality to experience, the mind is fully equipped to be immediately aware not only of the present self but of that other object which is causally ingredient in it. There is no need first to isolate the abstract notion of causality and then to make an inference from effect to cause; rather the abstract notion of causality is to be discovered by an analysis of the concrete reality of the immediate experience which embodies a causal relation.

§ 2

It is interesting to see what thinkers have developed a similar view of perception. Locke himself, although his formal theory of the knowledge of the external world is, as we have noticed, an inferential one, puts forward in treating of solidity considerations which might have led him to a more adequate doctrine. "If anyone asks me what this solidity is, I send him to his senses to inform him: let him put a flint or a football between his hands, and then endeavour to join them, and he will know."[1]

Of all philosophers it is Hamilton who has expressed this view of intuitive perception most clearly. His mature opinions have to be elicited from the dissertations appended to his edition of Reid rather than from his earlier *Lectures on Metaphysics*, and his language is unnecessarily pedantic, but he had a grasp of the matter which, although incomplete, no other philosopher has equalled. Between the primary and the secondary qualities as commonly distinguished, he singles out a group which he calls the secundo-primary qualities. These are the modes of the generic character of resistance, and through them we become aware of a spatial world outside our organism. For these qualities comprise both a subjective element as feelings and an objective element as manifestations of the resistance of an external body. The tactile feeling associated with pres-

[1] Locke: *Essay on the Human Understanding*, Bk. II, ch. iv, § 6.

sure Hamilton calls the secondary phasis of the secundo-primary quality of resistance, while its manifestation of an external body in the total or partial inhibition of movement on our part is its quasi-primary phasis.

"The existence of an extra-organic world is appre-hended, not in a perception of the Primary Qualities, but in a perception of the quasi-primary phasis of the Secundo-primary; that is, in the consciousness that our locomotive energy is resisted, and not resisted by aught in our organism itself. For, in the consciousness of being thus resisted is involved, as a correlative, the consciousness of a resisting something external to our organism. Both are, therefore, conjunctly appre-hended."[1]

There can be no doubt that Hamilton acknowledged a direct awareness of the external world, and conceived fairly accurately how this comes to be, although his mode of expression, when he speaks of consciousness of resistance, together with the awareness that the resistance is not from the organism itself, might to the unwary suggest the premisses of an inference. A similar shade of ambiguity is observable in his imitators. Ward adopts his general point of view and speaks of an intuition of the external world, but he is not altogether happily inspired when he describes this as "the projection of a subjectively determined exertion which meets with resistance, thereby making us acquainted with the occupation of space."[2] There is also a certain suggestion of inference in a statement like this of G. F. Stout, which nevertheless approximates to the truth.

"The experience of resisted effort supplies at once the most obvious and the most important example of the experienced contrast and correlation of external

[1] Hamilton's *Reid*, Note D*, p. 882.
[2] J. Ward: *Psychological Principles*, ch. vi, §6, 2nd ed., p. 163.

object and embodied self. The same complex sense-experience conditions the perception both of the bodily effort and of the correlative resistance. Inasmuch as it is variable through our own initiative, it yields the awareness of an effort which we ourselves are making. Inasmuch as it is variable independently of our subjective control, it yields the awareness of a resisting not-self. The resistance we naturally apprehend as proceeding from a counter-effort opposed to our own."[1]

Stout and Ward are plainly the heirs of Hamilton, and from a more independent point of view we may add to them A. N. Whitehead, with his vindication of the cognitive mode of causal efficacy as not less primitive than that of presentational immediacy. In criticizing Hume's view of perception, he remarks with justice that "Hume's argument first tacitly presupposes the two modes of perception, and then tacitly assumes that presentational immediacy is the only mode. Also Hume's followers, in developing his doctrine, presuppose that presentational immediacy is primitive, and that causal efficacy is the sophisticated derivative. This is a complete inversion of the evidence."[2] All these thinkers have shown genuine insight into the nature of perception; none of them have expressed it in completely unexceptionable terms or have provided a satisfactory analysis of the conditions of intuition.

§ 3

For an analysis of the conditions of intuitive perception we have to look back to the Aristotelian scholastics of the Middle Ages. In order to appreciate these thinkers, we have to place ourselves in a different intellectual

[1] G. F. Stout: *Mind and Matter*, Bk. IV, ch. i, 3, pp. 232–3.
[2] A. N. Whitehead: *Symbolism*, ch. ii, 5, p. 61.

atmosphere, in which a common-sense view of the external world was assumed and the critical problems of knowledge which have been the staple matter of discussion in modern philosophy had not yet been raised. Although their chief philosophical merits lie in more metaphysical territory, their analysis of perception is a much more important contribution to our present subject than has usually been realized. They had no doubt that the perception of the external world was intuitive; in fact they generally took for granted that the specific sense-qualities belonged to external objects. Now that the matter has received attention from philosophers, this assumption can no longer be upheld, and the mediaeval theory of perception needs to be supplemented by an analysis of the primitive data of consciousness which the scholastics did not undertake. Nevertheless their view of perception is, as we shall see, of permanent interest.

They all employed much the same language, but they did not all interpret it in precisely the same way. These divergences of interpretation have been analysed by G. Picard, who discovers two main systems of thought on the question of perception.[1] Picard endeavours in the end to bring these systems closer together, and to smooth out their differences; we, on the other hand, shall take the view that they are fundamentally divergent and irreducible, but the material which Picard provides for a judgment has still to be gratefully accepted.

The later opinion, whose typical representative is Suarez, holds that the act of knowing is essentially an assimilation of the subject to the object. *Actualis cognitio quaedam est actualis assimilatio.* In order that the subject's power of knowing should be actualized, it must be affected or determined in the appropriate way by the object; this determination, which is logically prior to the cognitive act, is called the *species impressa.* While the *species impressa* makes the assimilation of the subject to

[1] Cf. G. Picard: *Essai sur la Connaissance Sensible d'après les Scolastiques.*

the object possible, it is not itself an assimilation, for to be this is a property of the act of knowing. The *species impressa* is only *instrumentum quoddam ad ipsam actualem expressamque similitudinem formandam*. The cognitive act which follows is at the same time the production of a representative of the object, the *species expressa*, which, although it is not itself an object of knowledge except to further reflection, is the means by which the object is known.

This system of thought, which is the interpretation of the scholastic doctrine of *species* still adopted by many and presented to the inquirer as its proper meaning, is open to considerable objection. The description of knowing as the production of a likeness of the object, while it is a permissible metaphor, must, if literally accepted, bring about a regrettable materialization of the notion of knowing. The *species impressa*, if it is not itself an assimilation of the subject to the object, becomes an unintelligible piece of mental mechanism without content or relation to experience. Moreover, if all knowing produces a kind of image of the object, you may go on saying that the object is directly known through the image, and that the image is not the object of knowledge, but sooner or later you will begin to regard the image as the primary object of knowledge and to wonder how you can justify its ostensible reference to the external object. This is, of course, precisely what Descartes did, and it can hardly be denied that it is a natural development from a theory of perception of the Suarezian type.

When, however, we turn to Aquinas and the Thomistic school, we find something very different. All knowing takes place through the assimilation of the subject to the object (*omnis cognitio est per assimilationem cognoscentis ad cognitum*), but the formal assimilation does not reside in the act of knowing. Knowing is just knowing; it cannot be defined, and no analogy or metaphor will exhaust its nature. A *species impressa* is required when, as in perception, the object to be known is distinct from the subject. Then the subject must first be made like the object, and this assimilation is effected by the reception of the *species impressa* through the activity of the external object. The act of perception follows, and does not involve any *species expressa* or image of the object, for the object is itself directly present to the percipient and needs no representative in the cognitive act itself. There is occasion to speak of a *species expressa* only when the object is not directly present, as when we imagine something.

In spite of the similarity of language this is really a quite different theory of knowledge from that of Suarez. The notion of knowing is duly left to be appreciated in and for itself; it is not interpreted in terms of anything else. There is no fear that the thinker will be led into a doctrine of representative ideas, for in the act of direct perception there is no representation. The *species impressa* acquires meaning and content, for it is that assimilation of the subject to the object which is required in order that the subject may know something other than itself. In fact the assimilation of the subject to the object under the influence of the object is precisely the communication which we have been describing as the condition of intuitive perception. Supplemented by a preliminary account of the primitive data of consciousness, and applied with the restrictions demanded by the later analysis of sensation, the Thomistic view of perception might have been usefully taken into account by philosophers since Descartes.

§ 4

The knowledge of other minds raises questions similar to those involved in the perception of material things. For one who, like Locke, regards all perception as inferential, the belief in the existence of other minds must be based on an inference too. It is curious to see what

Berkeley makes of it, since, while denying material substance, he held firmly to the existence of other minds. We find that he maintains this belief to be inferential, and from the hasty paragraph which he devotes to the question it appears that this is an inference by analogy with the behaviour of the subject. "I perceive several motions, changes, and combinations of ideas, that inform me there are certain particular agents, like myself, which accompany them, and concur in their production."[1]

Reid, who asserts that there is intuitive perception of the material world, says also that there is a primitive belief, prior to reasoning, in the existence of other minds. He does not, however, seem altogether happy about the logical status of this belief, for he adds reasoning to it. "Setting aside this natural conviction, I believe the best reason we can give, to prove that other men are living and intelligent, is, that their words and actions indicate like powers of understanding as we are conscious of in ourselves."[2] He looks upon this reasoning as parallel to the teleological argument for the existence of God. In our own day H. H. Price gives a similar turn to the argument, finding its chief strength in the discernment in the world about us of purposive action which can only proceed from other minds.[3]

Certainly, given a perception of the material world, there can be an argument yielding rational assurance that some of the objects which surround us embody minds more or less like our own. It is not merely a question of similarity of appearance; this may be deceptive, as a visitor to a waxworks sometimes has occasion to notice. The real strength of the argument, as Reid and Price observe, is in the discernment of behaviour which presupposes sense-experience, in the case of animals, or sense-experience and thought, in the case

[1] Berkeley: *Principles of Human Knowledge*, § 145.
[2] Reid: *Essays on the Intellectual Powers*, essay VI, ch. v.
[3] H. H. Price: "Our Knowledge of Other Minds," in *Proceedings of the Aristotelian Society*, 1931–2, pp. 53–78.

of other men. We cannot fail to remark that our desires are constantly being assisted or thwarted in a way which would be unintelligible if the objects in the world about us which appear to possess sense-organs like our own did not in fact have sense-experience, or sense-experience together with thought.

An inference of this nature is probably the whole reason why we attribute sense-experience to animals; we do not seem to have any direct insight into the experience of animals, or people would not be so tempted to put an anthropomorphic construction upon their feelings and behaviour. It does not, however, appear that our knowledge of other human minds is always and exclusively inferential. That it is often inferential is evident, because it is fallible; it is very easy to misconstrue another person's thoughts and feelings. Yet there are occasions when we seem to have flashes of insight into the thoughts and feelings of another, and there is no sound reason to dismiss this appearance as illusory. Price admits that intuitive knowledge of other minds may sometimes be possible, but he thinks that such occasions are too rare to serve as a foundation for our everyday beliefs about other minds. The reasons which are given for an intuitive theory of the knowledge of other minds are often, no doubt, extremely unconvincing; they may be based, for example, on the notion that group-consciousness is more primitive than individual self-consciousness, which has a vague suggestiveness in relation to the psychology of primitive races, but can scarcely be upheld as literally true. Nevertheless, there may be a better reason for thinking that an intuitive knowledge of other minds occurs with fair frequency.

For, if the condition of perceptual intuition is assimilation or communication in the sense explained, it appears that this condition is quite frequently verified in our dealings with other human beings. Generally, no doubt, we are interpreting their words and expression in accordance with the habits set up in us by experience, and thereby forming an abstract conception of what they think and feel. Such an abstract conception cannot, of course, be a basis for intuition; intuition depends upon concrete communication. It not rarely happens, however, that our contact with other minds is closer, and we receive the sharp impression of the impact of other minds upon our own. This is when we begin, as we say, to see with their eyes; not only are abstract concepts but a concrete point of view, a whole way of thinking and feeling, is transferred momentarily from one mind to another. We do not merely contemplate in an abstract manner, from outside, what another person seems to be thinking; we find ourselves thinking and feeling with him, at least for a brief space of time. In this case the condition of concrete assimilation is fulfilled, and the special character of this kind of experience is really due to its being an intuitive awareness of another mind and not simply an inferential interpretation. Consequently, although the greater part of our knowledge of other minds is inferential, there are occasions when we have genuine intuitions of them, and such intuitions are probably the source of our earliest convictions of the reality of other minds.

The way in which communication between other minds and our own is brought about is, at least normally, through sensation and, therefore, through material channels. Whatever may be thought about telepathy, it is at any rate unusual. Hence our normal intuitive experience is of embodied minds. It is conceivable that disembodied minds should communicate with us, but this evidently does not appertain to the common state of terrestrial life.

§ 5

With the recognition of the external world the distinction ordinarily made between sensation and imagination becomes fully intelligible. In what is commonly called imagining two elements must be distinguished.

There is the image proper, which is a datum of the same nature as a sensation, although we call it an image because we attribute its origin to prior mental activity instead of to external stimulation. There is also the supposal of an external thing of the kind to which we should have attributed its origin if it had been a sensation. Thus, when we imagine a friend with us in the room, there is both a visual datum resembling that which we should have if he were really present and the intellectual supposal of him as being present in the room.

While we cannot be mistaken in believing that we have the datum which is the image proper, for this is a direct object of consciousness, we can be mistaken in believing that what is in fact a mere supposal is a real external thing. If you think you see a pink rat climbing up the curtain, you are right in thinking that you are conscious of a pink visual datum but wrong in attributing its origin to an animal climbing up the curtain. In practice we do not usually have much difficulty in distinguishing between sensation and imagination. We have a considerable spontaneous power of discrimination between those data towards which we feel passively receptive and those which we are actively producing. Moreover, we have an intuitive perception of those bodies with which we are in active contact. The visual data which we have learned to associate with these bodies we find to be in a certain continuity with other visual data, and these we take as the basis of perceptual inference to the existence of other bodies.

Sometimes, of course, it is only reasonable to remain in doubt. Did I hear that sound, or did I merely imagine it? Not all perceptual inferences, as opposed to perceptual intuitions, are of sufficient force to justify rational assurance; we need not be surprised if they are sometimes erroneous. Especially persistent and glaring errors of this kind we describe as hallucinations. Descartes, in the initial stages of his thinking, contemplated the possibility that all his perceptual beliefs were hallucinations.

Such a fear should not survive an adequate criticism of experience. A study of the victims of hallucination seems to show that they are deceived because they either cannot or will not consider rationally whether they are hallucinated. It is not that they coolly and dispassionately judge something to be real which is not real; rather they are inhibited, either by a sudden shock or by a permanent failure of mind, from considering and judging, and so they are hurried on to act as if the thing were real. If they could bring themselves to think coolly about it, they would understand that it was an illusion.

There is a parallel between hallucination and the ordinary experience of dreaming. When we are asleep, extrinsically stimulated experience is either absent or at a minimum; the imagination, therefore, may enjoy a freedom of exercise which it lacks in waking life. But we do not, while dreaming, genuinely judge that we are perceiving real things. When we are able to ask ourselves this question, we begin to wake up. When we are fully asleep, however, the question remains unasked. In the absence of genuine perception and of a genuine perceptual judgment, the dreamer's feelings and emotions proceed as if he were having perceptual experience. The wraith-like character which in our waking hours we recognize to belong to the life of dream is evidently due to the diminution or absence of that consciousness of the body and intuitive perception of neighbouring bodies which are the foundation of real perception.

In normal waking experience, therefore, we have certain unmistakable perceptual intuitions and a multitude of perceptual inferences of different degrees of reliability, not excluding complete rational assurance. Perceptual inferences deserve confidence as long as we retain critical control of our judgments. When we can ask ourselves coolly whether we are deceived or not, deception is not to be feared. Although, from time to time, we may make erroneous inferences, the general body of perceptual inference will be approximately correct.

## § 6

Memory provides us with direct knowledge of the continuing identity of the self, but we have no such direct knowledge of the identity of other things. We become aware of them not primarily in their substantial individuality but as the possessors of certain qualities and powers. The direct individual consciousness of the self remains unique.

Nevertheless we usually regard ourselves as capable of establishing the identity of things we perceive with things we remember, and it would be an abuse of language to deny to many instances of such belief the name of certainty. This certainty, however, is the result neither of immediate awareness nor of a simple demonstrative inference but of the convergence of a number of probable indications. When I come back to my study after going out for a while, I find the familiar desk, chairs and bookcases waiting for me, or rather, to be more exact, I find no observable difference between the desk, chairs and bookcases which I now perceive and those which I remember perceiving before I went out. Supposing, however, that someone during my absence had replaced one of these objects by a perfect replica, I should have no means of discovering the change by merely observing the object. It is even practically conceivable that someone, at some time since I last looked at one of my books, should have damaged it and taken advantage of my absence to replace it by a clean copy of the same edition. The book might then look exactly the same to me as the one which I had previously used. Hence we should be chary of claiming knowledge in the full sense of the term of the continuing identity of other bodies. Yet, in very many cases, it is impossible to suppose that any substitution has taken place; the evidence of identity is so complete in detail that we can only judge without hesitation that the thing is identical. This is to be certain, although with the kind of certainty which results from a convergence of probabilities.

The occurrence of this kind of certainty is especially evident in judgments about the identity of other persons. The absence of observable differences of appearance is not, of course, enough; we have all had difficulties with twins at one time or another. Yet the evidence of another person's remembered individual point of view, and of his memory of events which he alone could remember, is often, and indeed usually, so overwhelming that we suffer from no practical difficulty in recognizing without hesitation our friends and acquaintances. It would be wholly unreasonable to ask for more evidence of this than we in fact possess.

In general, a sound criticism of experience does not turn out to be the reversal of common sense which it has sometimes been feared to be; it is much more an analysis of what our common-sense beliefs are really about, and how we come to have them. We have maintained that we are conscious of ourselves in the present as substances and agents, possessing both bodily and mental properties, and experiencing transitory sensations. We have certain intuitions of our own past in memory, of external bodies with which we are in contact, and of other embodied minds. In addition we make many inferences in the fields of both memory and perception, and to these inferences we rationally attribute varying degrees of probability and even, in favourable cases, the kind of certainty which results from the convergence of probabilities. Any merely probable judgment may prove to be erroneous, but, if we preserve critical control, we shall at least know when we may be mistaken and shall be secure from falling into irremediable error.

# INDEX OF NAMES